LIBRARY PUBLIC RELATIONS, PROMOTIONS, AND COMMUNICATIONS

ual

S, INC.

New York, London

Published by Neal-Schuman Publishers, Inc.
100 Varick Street
New York, NY 10013

Printed and bound in the United States of America.

Library of Congress Cataloging-in-Publication Data

Wolfe, Lisa.
    Library public relations, promotions, and communications / by Lisa Wolfe.
        p.   cm.—(How-to-do-it manual ; no. 75)
Includes bibliographical references and index.
ISBN 1-55570-266-X
1. Public relations—Libraries—United States. I. Title. II. Series: How-to-do-it manuals for libraries ; no. 75.
Z716.3.W58   1997   IN PROCESS
021.7—dc21   97–1423

To Allan for his love, support, and the enforced solitude that helped me finish this book; to my mother and father for raising me to believe that I can do anything I set my mind to; and to the others who love and support me, and for whom I hope that I can always do the same—John, Sharon, Christy, and, of course, Samantha.

CONTENTS

FIGURES

PREFACE

In 1995, American Library Association President Arthur Curley called libraries "an American value." Indeed, many Americans view libraries as being "as American" as baseball and apple pie. This popular perception may be the reason so many people look quizzically at me when I tell them that I have dedicated my career to library public relations, promotions, and communications. They don't understand why libraries would pay anyone to tell their story to the public—they don't think libraries need to do public relations work at all.

I have had innumerable people tell me they think my job is making flyers for preschool storytimes. When city budgets get tight or when school districts have to make funding cuts, these same people express outrage that uninformed public officials call libraries "non-essential services." These librarians then rush to the media and their supporters for help in convincing the powers that be that quality library services are indeed essential. Some of these "crisis" media strategies are successful; others are not.

Typically, the successful libraries are those that have been telling their stories for years. They have developed strong programs and have worked hard to let their constituents know the value of library services. Then, when the day comes that those services need protection, there is an educated constituency that values the library and its services—constituents who not only see libraries as an American value, but who see their library as a *community* value.

THE IMPORTANCE OF TELLING THE LIBRARY STORY

As the saying goes, "there are a million stories in the naked city," and stories about what libraries accomplish must compete for the public's attention with those from sports, arts, other community and government entities, and private enterprise. The challenge is to make the library's story one that captures the public's attention and creates a positive perception of the library and its services. Planned public relations (PR) and communications efforts can help librarians meet this challenge. Building community support and becoming a regular positive focus for the local media takes time, energy, patience, knowledge, and skills.

Librarians often express frustration that their libraries don't get more media coverage and community support. When asked about their public relations/communications efforts, they reply that they have sent out one or two press releases or that they circulated a newsletter—to the same people who would use the library regularly whether there was a newsletter or not. Many libraries and librarians tend to be passive—expecting people to understand and value their services—rather than being proactive and telling their stories to their constituencies.

Libraries of all types have important stories to tell. Best of all, from a PR perspective, those stories can be centered around people—the public loves human interest stories, especially ones about people who triumph over adversity. Librarians can tell how their services and resources help build better lives. It is important to choose stories that would be interesting to you if you didn't work at the library. The public at large really isn't interested in the detailed specifications of the library's new shelving or the type of special steel it is made from. On the other hand, a story about how the new shelving was designed so that library users in wheelchairs can choose and take books from the shelves by themselves makes an interesting story—particularly if you can get wheelchair-confined users to talk about what this change means to them.

Sometimes libraries have a specific story that they want—or need—to tell, but every individual message must relate to the overall perception the library is trying to create among its constituencies. If you want people to think that your library is a warm, friendly place, then every message should have that "spin." If you want people to know that your library has serious budgetary problems, then all your communications efforts should emphasize how you are doing so much with so little.

The maxim in advertising is that people need to hear something three times before the message is really heard. Listen to radio or television commercials and pay attention to how many times the name of the product or company being promoted is said and/or displayed on the screen. People need to hear or read the same thing, over and over again, before that message becomes a part of their personal reality. Private enterprises never stop telling their stories—because they don't want people to stop buying their products. Likewise, we must never stop telling the library story; we don't want people to stop using and supporting our services.

By developing a public relations/communications plan that focuses on key messages and audiences, librarians can share their stories, increase public understanding of the value of library services, and, ultimately, increase financial support for library services and programs.

USING THIS BOOK TO DEVELOP, IMPLEMENT, AND EVALUATE A COMMUNICATIONS PLAN

Library Public Relations, Promotions, and Communications: A How-to-Do-It Manual provides an introduction to the basic communications concepts, a step-by-step process for developing and implementing a library public relations/communications plan, and descriptions of effective library communications tools and strategies. The first three chapters focus on the theory and planning process for public relations and communications, the next ten chapters provide tools and strategies, and the final chapter will assist you in evaluating your efforts.

Detailed examples of the application of solid communications planning in school, public, academic, and special libraries are included throughout the book. They show those struggling with how to "get the word out" some effective strategies for achieving their goals. Each example demonstrates that a clear communications goal and a plan for achieving it are the key components to success in your public relations efforts. Each chapter also includes samples and guiding questions to assist you in carefully evaluating the available communications resources and in developing a strategy for using those resources to reach your library's audience and communicate your message.

Chapter 1, "Thinking About Communications and Public Relations For Your Library," introduces the vocabulary used in the world of public relations. It explains the differences and similarities among the concepts "public relations," "communications," "marketing," and "promotion." The chapter will also help you think about why your library needs a public relations plan and how you can identify the human and fiscal resources needed—and that might be available—to implement your plan.

The planning process for your library's public relations/communications efforts is detailed in Chapter 2, "Developing Your Library's Public Relations/Communications Plan." By following each step in this chapter, you will determine your library's public relations goal, identify your message and audience, and formulate specific objectives and strategies. A series of questions is included to guide your thinking about your library's communications goal, message, and audience; sample plans also help you envision what your library's plan might look like.

Two of the most important components of effective communications efforts are given special attention in Chapter 3, "Defining Your Library's Message and Audience." The guiding questions included in this chapter are designed to help you focus on a specific communications message for your library and in targeting the appropriate audiences with that message.

In Chapter 4, "Developing a Corporate Identity for Your Library," the development of the tools for implementing your library's public relations/communications plan begins as you establish a corporate identity or "look" for your library. This chapter includes specific information on the elements of a corporate identity and the strategies for working with designers and printers.

Now that you have established your library's corporate identity, Chapter 5, "Creating Effective Print Communications," takes you through the process of planning, budgeting, and scheduling your library's publications. It will help you decide whether your printing and design can be done in-house or whether they should be contracted out, and it provides tips for working with printers and designers. The development process for effective newsletters, brochures, and annual reports is described in detail. Sample publication planning forms, schedules, and design and proofing checklists are included.

Chapter 6, "Expanding Your Library's Media Coverage," helps you increase and manage your library's press coverage. Strategies are presented for working and developing a relationship with reporters to get the good word out and to ensure that not-so-positive stories are presented in a balanced way. Time-saving processes for preparing news releases and public service announcements—and samples for both—are included. I also describe effective methods for using press conferences, press kits, video news releases, and cable-access television to tell your library's story to the community.

Volunteers can be an integral part of your library's communications effort. Chapter 7, "Telling Your Story Through Volunteers," will help you organize and manage a volunteer program for your library. Sample volunteer job descriptions are included. In addition, using children and teenagers as volunteers and the benefits of forming a Friends group are discussed.

Chapter 8, "Using Community Involvement as a Public Relations Tool," provides you with strategies for moving your library's public relations efforts "beyond the walls" of your library by using your best public relations tool—your staff. Recommendations are presented for encouraging library staff to get involved in the greater community and a sample application form for community involvement support is included. I also describe how to create a staff speakers bureau and think creatively about how your library can participate in community events.

The subtle messages that your library communicates are covered in Chapter 9, "Creating an Environment that Supports Your Message." Valuing and rewarding staff and creating a physical environment that communicates your library's message are the chapter's primary focus. The information in this chapter will help you to ensure that the reality of your library is consistent with your public relations message.

Electronic resources are another way to get the word out and Chapter 10, "Using Technology to Tell Your Library's Story," deals with them in detail. Listservs, e-mail, Web pages, newsgroups, and electronic bulletin board services are described and strategies for using them as part of your library's public relations program are suggested.

Programs and special events can be part of a library's communications plan as well as its service; as described in Chapter 11, "Programs and Special Events as Communications Tools," both tell the library's story and encourage people to visit the library. Definitions of programs and special events, planning forms and checklists, sample evaluation forms, and hints for encouraging sponsorships of your special event are included. The chapter also has information about how to use exhibits and displays as a communications tool.

Chapter 12, "Creating a Professional Network," provides you with the resources for making connections with those who do public relations work in libraries and other organizations. Opportunities for involvement in state and national library organizations as well as local and national public relations/communications organizations are described, and strategies for developing informal networking opportunities are presented. Information about entering contests and winning awards for your public relations efforts is also provided.

While the entire book includes examples and information for public, school, special, and academic librarians, Chapter 13, "Public Relations Challenges in Different Types of Libraries," focuses specifically on the unique obstacles and opportunities that each type of library faces. Success stories from school, public, special, and academic libraries are presented and the challenges that each type of library has had to grapple with are discussed.

The last chapter, Chapter 14, "Evaluating Your Efforts," reminds you that your public relations efforts are cyclical and never-ending. Guiding questions for evaluating your efforts in addition to strategies for using your public relations/communications plan as an evaluation tool are included.

This book includes the information and tools needed to develop and implement an ongoing public relations/communications plan for any type of library. When you get to Chapter 14 and are evaluating your efforts, you will find that the next step is to go right back to Chapter 2 and begin planning again. Each time you go through the process, your efforts will become more focused and you will have greater success.

Public relations is a building process. By implementing carefully planned public relations/communications activities, librarians in all types of libraries can inform and educate their constituencies and garner support for current programs and services as well as for future plans. Library public relations efforts don't have to be expensive or sophisticated in order to be successful, but they do have to be planned and implemented in a thoughtful manner to provide clear, consistent messages to the appropriate audiences.

I hope you will find *Library Public Relations, Promotions, and Communications* a valuable resource in your effort to tell your library's story.

1 THINKING ABOUT PUBLIC RELATIONS AND COMMUNICATIONS FOR YOUR LIBRARY

In these days when every government entity is competing for a shrinking tax dollar, people are looking critically at where those dollars are going. Public libraries compete with fire and police departments, parks, and even school districts. School libraries compete for dollars within their school districts and their buildings. Parents and school board members want to know why you still need a full-time school library media specialist when you have spent so much money on technology. You may consider that a silly question, but they don't—and for programs and positions to survive, that audience is going to need information to help build its understanding. Librarians and regular library users recognize the inherent value of library services, but other people usually don't.

Several years ago, a public library system was considering whether or not it could afford to continue providing outreach services to inmates at the county jail. The library system approached the county commissioners to ask for funding from the county to continue the service. One of the commissioners, who also happened to be a surgical nurse, suggested that perhaps the service could be continued using volunteers instead of library staff. A community member testifying at the hearing remarked, "Perhaps when the hospital budget gets into trouble, it could just use volunteers for some surgical services." Obviously, that person had developed an understanding of the value of professional librarians and trained, experienced paraprofessionals, and knew that library service is more than just checking out books. The citizen's analogy convinced the commissioner to vote to authorize funding for the service. Such a crucial understanding doesn't just happen; support like that comes from a well-planned and well-executed public relations program.

PLANNING FOR PUBLIC RELATIONS

Summer reading happens every year at Anytown Public Library and every year the staff does the same things to promote it — news releases, flyers, children's librarians visiting school classrooms. Every year, the program is implemented, attendance is average, circulation increases slightly, and by the end of August, the children's librarians are exhausted. There was never a written public relations plan for summer reading and the efforts were never evaluated. No one ever sat down and thought about how the promotion of summer reading fits into the rest of the library's public relations efforts. While they may be doing exactly what works, they might not be getting the most effectiveness from their efforts or the most bang for their buck.

By carefully planning the summer reading promotion and considering where it fits in the library's overall public relations efforts, Anytown Public Library will be able to achieve better results and make their limited dollars go further. Evaluating their efforts based on the plan will help them improve their strategies for next year. For example, perhaps if they look at all the other public relations activities in the library, they may discover that three other activities are being heavily promoted with the local media during the same time period as summer reading. That may provide an answer to the children's librarians constant query, "We are doing really creative programs. Why don't we ever get any news coverage?" Library-wide planning will help Anytown Public Library avoid competing with itself for news coverage or other types of public attention.

In your library, a public relations/communications plan will also be a guide as you get involved in the hectic pace of working on your project. By referring to the plan, you can see what you have done, what you need to do, and (based on the experiences you have had thus far, and your timing or budget constraints) what elements of your plan might need to be changed. You have a record of where your time and energy have gone and you can evaluate your efforts and decide where they might be best directed in the future.

Above all, developing your library's public relations/communications plan forces you to sit down and think about where you have been, where you are going, and what you want to do. It gives you a reason to consider thoughtfully the communications tools available to you and how to use them.

You will have to decide whether to do a comprehensive or a project-based public relations plan. Several factors should influence your decision. If this is your first public relations effort, a project plan may be the best place to start. You can build on that with future efforts. If you are in a library where lots of project-based public relations efforts—planned or not—are already occurring, a comprehensive plan is probably what you want to develop. It will provide an opportunity to bring the various activities into one cohesive and complementary effort. Be careful when deciding what kind of plan to develop not to take on more than you can handle. Set yourself up for success by developing a goal and a plan that are manageable based on your experience and fiscal and human resources.

Planning will put your public relations efforts into a context where they will support your overall program rather than derail it or contradict it. Planning will make the process of telling your story and garnering public understanding more efficient, more effective, and more fun!

STAFFING FOR PUBLIC RELATIONS

Once you have decided that planned public relations/communications is a priority for your library, it is critical that one person be designated to coordinate implementation of your plan. This doesn't mean that one person has to do everything, but it is necessary to have a lead person who oversees the plan's implementation and follows up on the completion of scheduled activities.

A public relations staff, or at least one full-time person devoted to managing your public relations, is the ideal. There are two schools of thought about what a public relations manager's training or background should be. Some maintain that only a professional librarian can accurately represent the library's philosophy, programs, and services. Others hold that it is most important for a library public relations manager to have a background in public relations, communications, or journalism. Probably the perfect person for the job would be a librarian with a background in public relations. Whoever you hire should be an effective communicator, who is well organized with creative ideas and lots of energy, and who understands and believes in the value of library service.

As stated above, a full-time public relations staff is ideal for many libraries, particularly larger public libraries and academic libraries. However, the ideal may not always be practical when other budget and staffing needs are taken into consideration. You may have to reassign the duties of a current staff person so that person can spend a portion of his or her time working on your library's public relations program. If you have decided that public relations is a priority for your library, it is critical that the person appointed receive release time from regular duties in order to handle public relations activities. Your public relations efforts will not be effective if they are merely added to a staff member's already massive workload. By freeing up staff time to work on public relations and by devoting human resources to your efforts, you are making a statement about your library's commitment to telling its story.

For school library media specialists, public relations may indeed be another job responsibility in an already unmanageable workload. You can, however, think about what tasks, including some of the public relations activities, can be delegated to volunteers. Creating a relationship with public relations/communications staff at the school district level is another way to lighten your load. Such a relationship also provides you with an opportunity to see where your building or departmental plans fit within the school district's overall public relations plan.

Academic librarians may have some of the same opportunities for shifting workloads that public librarians have. And like school librarians they have the opportunity to work closely with the college or university's public relations office to coordinate efforts.

Again, however you staff your public relations activities, one key person should coordinate and oversee all efforts so that your library takes a big-picture approach.

Another staffing related issue to consider is who will supervise the public relations person. Whether you have a full-time public relations person or a staff member who is coordinating your efforts on a part-time basis, the chain of command for this person could have a significant impact on the success of your plan. In the corporate world, public relations directors often report directly to the chief executive officer. If they aren't direct reports, they typically have direct access to that person. The reason for this relationship is obvious: it is always important that the person telling the organization's story receive a clear message from the top about what that story is. A library's public relations efforts and the goals of its administration must be tightly interwoven and not working at cross-purposes. A public relations person who reports to the library director knows the organizational priorities and can follow them. When competing priorities are presented, the public relations person has the ability to say, "The library director said we are going to do it this way." That kind of clout can be very to important to effective public relations.

In a school environment, the principal should have a clear understanding of the school library media specialist's public relations efforts. The principal might even participate in the implementation of public relations activities. Such support speaks loudly to the rest of the faculty, to parents, and to school board members about the importance of the school library media program. It also provides the school librarian with help in reshaping job duties so that he or she can devote some time to public relations activities. A school librarian with a strong interest in public relations should garner the support of the district public relations person—and perhaps even volunteer to serve on a district-wide public relations advisory committee or to work on district-wide public relations activities. Such activities provide more chances to tell the library's story from a district-wide public relations perspective.

Again, the academic librarian's situation is a combination of that of public and school librarians. The person responsible for public relations in a college or university library should report to the library director for that part of his or her duties, but a strong relationship with the college or university's public relations staff is also necessary. Volunteering to be involved with institution-wide public relations efforts is a good strategy for an academic librarian; such involvement provides a broader perspective and offers opportunities for integrating the library into the institution's overall public relations efforts.

The most important thing about choosing staff for your library's public relations efforts is to look for someone who is passionate about your library's services, programs, and role in the community, and who has the ability to communicate that passion. A person with these qualities will be able to recruit volunteers for your efforts, garner staff support for the importance of public relations, and, ultimately, achieve your public relations goals.

THE VALUE OF COLLABORATION

While it is important to have a person who takes lead responsibility for your library's public relations activities, planning and implementation of public relations and communications should be a collaborative effort among the library staff and volunteers—even if they only serve in an advisory capacity. You may want to form a library-wide task force or committee to plan your public relations efforts, and then involve the same group or a new one in implementing and evaluating the plan.

Other library staff will bring significant concerns and information to your communications activities but involvement of a wide variety of staff will also encourage all of the staff to take ownership in your efforts. Public relations activities may be something that your principal or library board has asked you to become involved with, possibly causing difficulties for staff in general—more work, additional confusion in the middle of a busy workday, and the need to drop everything to help you deal with reporters. It is important that all staff understand the value of what you are doing *before* public relations activities interrupt their work schedules. For example, if your communications planning committee members agree that unless you get the word out and increase your library's circulation statistics and gate count, the city council is going to cut your budget in the next fiscal year, library staff who serve on the committee will understand that dropping everything to help you deal with a reporter isn't an interruption of their work, but rather a key to their survival. Staff who serve on the planning committee for communications activities will develop such an understanding and be committed to your efforts. In addition, they can share their commitment with their coworkers.

Serving on a planning or advisory committee can be an excellent educational opportunity for library staff. Front-line staff will learn more about the challenges of getting the word out, while you learn more about what really happens at a public service desk. One example of a communications activity that could have proved problematic if not for the "buy in" of front-line staff involved a public library that was asked by a radio station to help in a promotion. The radio station was giving away free tickets to a Rolling Stones concert by hiding them in various places around the city and then giving its listeners clues to finding them. The station's promotions manager approached the library's communications director and asked to hide tickets in a book at the library. This was an excellent opportunity to promote the library—particularly to the radio station's listeners, ages 20 to 40—and it created an image of the library as a fun, hip place. The communications director agreed, but there was a catch—she wasn't allowed to tell anyone because the hiding place was a secret. On the morning that the clue was announced on the air, over 100 people were waiting for the library to open. They ran into the building and began looking for the book where the tickets were hidden. The staff stood helplessly by and looked befuddled. The tickets were found and the chaos ended.

The library staff could have been upset about not being forewarned. But, after years of successful communications activities and many library staff serving on various communications planning and advisory committees, the majority of the staff recognized the opportunity and understood why the communications director had taken advantage of it. They were quick to squelch the complaints of the "naysayers." The process of education and buy-in that had taken place over nearly a 10-year period had paid off—and both the staff and the radio station's listeners had a little bit of fun while spreading the word about the public library.

Another reason to involve other library staff in your efforts is that in most cases you alone cannot implement your plans. For example, if you are trying to increase use of your academic library's Internet services by community members, you can develop and promote training events, but you will need to work with a variety of people—the library's technology coordinator to plan and implement the training, the custodian to set up the room for the training sessions, and perhaps the circulation manager if you are going to offer community members free library cards when they come for the training. While the goal of this project might be to change community members' perception about the university and the role that it can play in their neighborhood, it will take a collaborative effort to plan, promote, and implement this activity that was developed in support of your goal.

FUNDING YOUR EFFORTS

True commitment to library public relations will mean choosing to spend money on public relations. Once your plan is developed, you will need a budget to support it. If you can't afford what you planned, then hard decisions must to be made and your plan will need to be pared back or alternative funding sources, such as grants, will have to be investigated. The problem with grants, or "soft" money, is that they go away; if your public relations efforts are funded entirely by grant funds, when the grant is over, so are your public relations activities. When you make public relations a priority, a separate budget for those efforts is important to your success. It doesn't have to be a huge amount of money, but it must be realistic in terms of what you are planning to do. Two to five percent of your overall library budget is often a good target.

When you are convincing your library board, school-based management team, or university library director that this is an important expenditure, think about trying to place a value on the results of the public relations efforts. Of a $2 million budget, $100,000 will seem like a drop in the bucket if it has the potential to increase public support and pass an upcoming bond issue of $40 million, or to increase your circulation to such an extent that the city council will appropriate an extra $1 million for your library budget next year. On a different level, $250 out of a school library media center's $5,000 budget might not seem like much to spend on public relations efforts, but, school and academic libraries may have the opportunity to build on the overall public relations efforts of their school districts or universities. The important thing is to make a commitment to a level of spending for public relations that is commensurate with your overall library budget, and to consider that commitment as important as any other line item in your budget. Some day your public relations/communications efforts may be critical to your library's very survival.

A word of warning is in order, however. Your public relations plan has the potential to achieve great things for your library, but there are no guarantees. It is an obvious gamble for those making the funding decisions. If you have a detailed public relations plan, however, and ask for a reasonable amount of money based on that plan, you have a better chance of having your budget request granted and of achieving your public relations goals, so that you can return the next year with bigger goals, a bigger plan, and possibly a request for more funding.

DEFINITION OF TERMS

The terms public relations, marketing, promotion, and advertising are used frequently and often interchangeably in the profit and nonprofit worlds, including the library community. While these terms are all communications strategies, however, they are not interchangeable. Before you can develop a successful public relations/communications plan, clear definitions of these terms are needed. Not only will these definitions help you design a plan that is most appropriate for your library's needs, they will help you when you sell the plan to other staff, and to board and community members.

You can find similar definitions like the following in your dictionary. They will give you a place to begin thinking about public relations, marketing, promotion, and advertising as distinct but overlapping concepts.

Public relations: the business of trying to convince the public to have understanding for and goodwill toward a person, firm, or institution; *also*: the degree of understanding and goodwill achieved.

Marketing: 1: actually selling or purchasing in a market 2: a combination of functions involved in moving goods from producer to consumer.
Promotion: trying to further the growth or development of something; *esp*: trying to sell merchandise through advertising, publicity, or discounting.
Advertising: Calling something to the attention of the public, especially by paid announcements.

None of these terms is a new concept; the etymologies date the origin of the term "advertising" to 1762 and "marketing" to 1561. "Public relations" is the newest—having been coined in 1807. Yet, as a result of our increasingly competitive marketplace, particularly in the area of information services, they should be and are becoming more and more a part of our society's common vocabulary. And, during the current information explosion, understanding and application of these concepts is key to the future of library services in this country, particularly for school and public libraries.

Figure 1.1 illustrates the relationships among these complex concepts. As you can tell, none of them can really exist without at least one of the others and they are all required for effective marketing. The diagram demonstrates the idea that public relations, marketing, promotion, and advertising used in any combination are all interrelated "communication" activities.

PUBLIC RELATIONS

In 1975, the Foundation for Public Relations Research had 65 leaders in the profession write their own definition for public relations.

> Public relations is a distinctive management function which helps establish and maintain mutual lines of communication, understanding, acceptance and cooperation between an organization and its publics; involves the management of problems or issues; helps management keep informed on and responsive to public opinion; defines and emphasizes the responsibility of management to serve the public interest; helps management keep abreast of and effectively utilize change, serving as an early warning system to help anticipate trends; and uses research and sound and ethical communications techniques as its principal tools. [1]

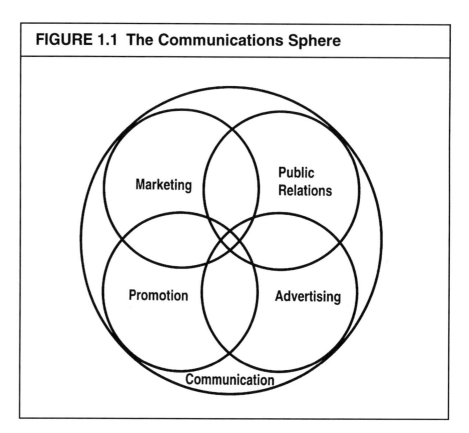

FIGURE 1.1 The Communications Sphere

Marketing

Public Relations

Promotion

Advertising

Communication

This comprehensive definition may sound complicated, but basically public relations works to create positive perceptions of your library. It is related to marketing when it is being used as part of a marketing plan, but it also exists in its own right as a critical tool for creating goodwill toward your library and its services. At times, public relations is reactive. For example, if the local newspaper is writing a story on the new circulating video collection at your library, it is your job to make sure that the reporter puts a positive spin on this new service. The reporter may want to talk about how the library is now competing with private enterprise—the video store on the corner. In order to have a story that creates a positive perception of your library and its programs, you need to work with the reporter to ensure that he or she accurately reflects the purpose of the video collection, understands the importance of providing information in a variety of formats, and still gets a story that will be interesting to readers. This is not a simple challenge. Chapter 6 deals with learning how to work effectively with the media. Effective media relations are an important part of positive public relations.

At other times, public relations is proactive. For example, if your university library will now be open 24 hours, you may want the campus newspaper to do a positive article that stresses the security measures that will be part of your late-night open hours. By encouraging news coverage of your new open hours, you also risk criticism. Perhaps the reporter will interview students who will say that they feel the library is not safe and secure during your daytime open hours and that they would never feel safe there at night. The students may or may not be telling the truth—perhaps they are just anxious to be quoted in the campus newspaper. Nevertheless, you have a media opportunity that could become a negative one if you don't handle it correctly. Again, working effectively with the reporter to tell your story is important for successful proactive public relations.

Good public relations plans include multiple approaches to achieving their goals. They acknowledge the different ways of reaching an audience and the diversity within even a clearly delineated audience. For example, if you want community members of ages 30 to 45 to learn about and understand the importance of continuing to fund library service to the elderly in nursing homes, and if you know that your target demographic group reads the local newspaper, you might try to have the paper run a human interest story about this service. That is one approach to achieving your goal, but it should be only one component of your overall plan for communicating the message. Other components might include working with a local talk radio station with the appropriate demographics to do a story that includes interviews of elderly people who value your service; launching a television public service announcement campaign of spots with nursing home patrons talking about what library services mean to them; or even developing a volunteer program so that community members can join your staff on their monthly visits to the nursing homes. In concert, these components could create a multidimensional public relations plan for reaching your goal.

In order to be most effective, public relations efforts should be time intensive—they should happen in a concentrated period of time. For example, in the approach described above, the efforts will have the greatest impact if they occur within two to three months rather than two to three years. The messages we remember most are the ones we hear at least three times within a limited time frame. If the time during which you plan to reach your goal is too long, your message will be obscured by other messages.

Careful planning is extremely important for successful public relations. This doesn't preclude taking advantage of serendipitous opportunities, like an offer from a television station to produce free public service announcements that further your efforts.

In fact, such opportunities will be even more meaningful if your library has a clear overall plan for public relations. Careful planning means that you and the other staff will all have a clear road map toward your public relations goal and will be able to concentrate efforts on reaching that goal rather than taking a scattershot approach. It will help you develop clear, consistent messages to deliver over and over again to your constituency. A plan also provides you with a mechanism for evaluating your efforts.

Ironically, public relations has developed a somewhat negative reputation. P. T. Barnum is sometimes referred to as "the father of public relations" and his trademark, "There's a sucker born every minute," has dogged the practice of public relations and public relations practitioners for years. Public relations practitioners have been referred to as "spin doctors" and "flacks." Our increasingly sophisticated society tends to be suspicious of public relations. Libraries are viewed by many as institutions that should be above the kind of practices that the negative connotations surrounding public relations imply. Yet, thoughtful taxpayers can be convinced that their tax dollars for library programs and services will be ill-spent if the community doesn't know about and understand those services. Unfortunately, though, the first step in your library's public relations plan might need to be creating a positive public perception of the importance of public relations for libraries, especially if you are planning to devote significant human or fiscal resources to your effort.

John Cotton Dana is considered the father of library public relations. Dana, a librarian who pioneered using public relations to promote library use, was the first director of the Newark museum, the first president of the Special Libraries Association, and the 11th president of the American Library Association. He established the first children's room and the first U.S. branch library for the business community. Since 1946, the American Library Association has annually presented the John Cotton Dana Library Public Relations Award for outstanding library public relations.[2]

Positive public perception of the library is more important than high gate counts or circulation when you need the community's help in funding a new service or the school board's support for increased materials budgets for the school library media program. A good example of this is a public library board member who served for more than eight years. He readily admitted that he didn't use the library's services—he bought his books. But he dedicated countless volunteer hours to his work on the board and to the library's capital campaign. Why? He said he recognized the importance of high-quality library service in a community—even if he didn't use it himself. He never added to the gate count or the circulation statistics, but he made a significant contribution to that library's success.

Developing positive perceptions of a school, public, or academic library does not happen overnight. And while public relations involves working to create that perception, it is critical that the reality the public faces when they come to use your services matches the positive perception you've instilled in your community.

MARKETING

Marketing seems to be today's buzzword in terms of library promotion. Many library directors talk about developing marketing plans, when what they really need to develop is a public relations or communications plan. Public relations and promotion are both components of a comprehensive marketing plan, but they don't necessarily involve the intensive market research and study that marketing requires. In libraries, marketing might be used to influence a citizen's behavior, rather than just change his or her perception of the library. For example, a marketing campaign might be used to get citizens to check more videos out of the library. You would do research to discover what kind of videos the public wants, you would purchase them, and then promote them. The goal of a public relations campaign, on the other hand, can be simply to create a positive public perception of your library.

In fact, the corporate world acknowledges the value of including public relations as part of corporate communications. In his book *The Marketer's Guide to Public Relations*, Thomas Harris coins the term "Marketing Public Relations." He cites a number of corporate successes (such as the Cabbage Patch Kids phenomenon, the sale of Reese's Pieces candy following the release of the film *E.T.*, and Pillsbury's increased sales after its annual Bake-Off), as examples of corporate marketing goals that were met by public relations efforts. He defines marketing public relations as "the process of planning, executing and evaluating programs that encourage purchase and consumer satisfaction through credible communication of information and impressions that identify companies and their products with the needs, wants, concerns and interests of consumers."[3] Based on that definition, the public relations efforts of your library will often be marketing public relations. By creating the positive public perception of your library, you will encourage your public to use your services.

Comprehensive marketing begins before the service is developed or at a time when changing the service can be considered. Marketing begins with the identification of customer needs. If people don't need what you are planning to provide, there is no market. Through careful analysis of the results of market research, library services or collections are designed and promoted to the customer. The goal of marketing in the for-profit world is increased profits. In the library world, the goal might be increased circulation, gate count, or program attendance.

This is a rather simplistic description of a complex concept. For a more in-depth description of how to develop and implement a marketing plan, *Marketing: A How-to-Do-It Manual for Librarians* (Neal-Schuman, 1992), by Suzanne Walters, provides a step-by-step guide for using marketing to develop library services uniquely suited for your customers.

PROMOTION AND ADVERTISING

Promotion and advertising are terms that are also used interchangeably. Advertising, however, is a component of promotion, marketing, and public relations. For the purpose of this discussion, advertising will be limited to something you must purchase, such as television advertising spots that you purchase time for, ads that you place in the local newspaper, and billboards that you rent. If you have the budget to purchase advertising, it may be an effective public relations/communications strategy for your library. In addition, most outlets that sell advertising (such as newspapers, television and radio stations, transit advertising, and billboard rental companies) offer nonprofit rates that your library might be eligible for. Unreserved space is sometimes available *gratis* if you produce the artwork for the advertisement.

Promotional efforts can be part of your public relations/communications plan. When you promote a service or program, you are usually trying to cause people to act. For example, you promote preschool storytime so that people will bring their children. It isn't enough for them simply to know about storytime and think it is a good thing; you are trying to get them to participate. As another example, you might have a regular plan for promoting new titles in your collection—so that people visit the library, check out materials, and increase your circulation count.

You may decide that promotion and/or advertising will be important parts of your library's overall public relations efforts. Or you may decide to focus all your energy on simply creating a positive perception of your library without necessarily encouraging people to act on that perception. It doesn't matter which decision you make. However, it is critical that you think carefully about your goals and develop an overall plan that will help you meet those goals. In the next chapter, you will learn how to assess what you want to achieve and how to develop a plan for getting there.

CONCLUSION

By picking up this book, you have indicated that you are thinking about library public relations. At this point, you may even think that public relations is indeed something that you need to pursue. Deciding to commit the resources necessary to make communications a priority for your library will be the next step. Then, you will need to develop a detailed plan for your efforts. This plan will help you to identify your message and your communications goal, and to think carefully about the activities that will help you to achieve your goal.

As you explore developing effective public relations, promotions, and communications for libraries, you will learn that the definitions for public relations, marketing, promotion, and advertising are not clear-cut and that there is a lot of overlap and ambiguity. The following example from *Promoting Issues & Ideas: A Guide to Public Relations for Nonprofit Organizations* sums up the vagueness of the distinctions:

If the circus is coming to town and you paint a sign saying "Circus Coming to the Fairground Saturday," that's advertising. If you put the sign on the back of an elephant and walk him into town, that's promotion. If the elephant walks through the mayor's flower bed, that's publicity. And if you can get the mayor to laugh about it, that's public relations. [4]

NOTES

1. Scott M. Cutlip, Allen H. Center, and Glen M. Broom, *Effective Public Relations*, 6th ed. (Englewood Cliffs, N.J.: Prentice Hall, 1985), 4.
2. Connie Vinita Dowell, "A Revamped John Cotton Dana PR Award Turns 50," *American Libraries* 26 (October 1995):908–911.
3. Thomas L. Harris, *The Marketer's Guide to Public Relations* (New York: John Wiley & Sons, 1991), 12.
4. Public Interest Public Relations, *Promoting Issues and Ideas: A Guide to Public Relations for Nonprofit Organizations* (New York: The Foundation Center, 1987), 1.

2 DEVELOPING YOUR LIBRARY'S PUBLIC RELATIONS/ COMMUNICATIONS PLAN

Many organizations take the same approach to their communications efforts that Mickey Rooney and Judy Garland brought to planning theatrical productions in their 1940s movies. They say, "Let's do a newsletter, let's do flyers, let's do a news release"— just as Mickey and Judy used to say, "Let's do a show!" And, just as in those old movies, they may have the resources to produce those materials, but those communications tools may not be the best use of those resources in light of the communications goal. Without a careful plan that includes a clear goal, consistent message, and targeted audience, producing a newsletter, developing a brochure, or even launching a home page on the World Wide Web, are not public relations. And without coordinating these types of communications efforts, you can, at times, do more harm than good.

CLARIFYING YOUR LIBRARY'S PUBLIC RELATIONS GOAL

You probably have some idea—no matter how vague—of what you want to achieve with your public relations efforts. Answering the following questions in the next section may help you to clarify your public relations goal.

1. What is it that you want to tell people?
This is your message. You need to determine what it is you want people to know or understand. Often your message will have a quality that is more subjective than just conveying information. For instance, you won't just want people to know about your

books-by-mail service—you'll also want them to believe that it is a valuable community service. At other times, you will just want to convey information, such how the library's new overdue policy works. It is important to try to keep your message as simple and focused as possible.

2. Who do you want to tell?

Determining the audience for your message is critical to your success. Think about who needs to know what you are communicating. If your message is preschool storytime hours, then your primary audience is parents of preschoolers and your secondary audience may be day-care providers. Deciding who needs to receive your message will help you determine how to communicate it. Remember to consider your internal audiences. Chapter 5 provides an in-depth discussion of choosing your audience.

3. When do you want to communicate your message?

Timing is everything. Trying to spread the word about school library services is probably more appropriate during the school year than during the summer when families, teachers, and students aren't focused on school. If you are promoting an event, it is important to communicate your message intensively in a concentrated time period before the event. Sometimes it may take you longer to plan your public relations/communications efforts than to implement them.

4. Why do you want to tell people about this? Do you want them to do anything?

These questions go back to the subjective nature of your message. Once people learn about what you are trying to communicate, do you need them to act? Is this a proactive message? Do you want them to attend an event? Actively support the retention of a library service? Vote for supplemental funding?

Look carefully at your answers to these questions. They should form the foundation for a public relations goal. Remember that a goal should include a statement of what you want to achieve, delineate a time frame for achieving it, and indicate how you are going to measure your success.

Figures 2.1–2.3 provide examples of using the above questions to formulate a public relations/communications goal. Look carefully at each example and you will see how easy it is to formulate a public relations/communications goal. The answers to the questions can be turned into a measurable and focused goal statement. Spend thoughtful time answering the questions and

---

FIGURE 2.1 Formulating a Public Relations/Communications Goal: School Library

1. What is it that you want to tell people?

   We want to tell people Internet services in our school library media center would enhance learning for our students.

2. Who do you want to tell?

   Parents, teachers, and school board members

3. When do you want to communicate your message?

   Spring 1997

4. Why do you want to tell people about this? Do you want them to do anything?

   We want to do this so that the school board will approve funding for phone lines and an Internet provider.

Goal: Communicate to parents, teachers, and school board members the role that the Internet can play in education for children. Demonstrate the Internet's valuable educational resources in order to secure funding for Internet services in the school library-media center by June 1997.

---

formulating your goal. It will be the foundation on which you build your plan and it is important to your success that you clearly articulate what you want to achieve.

COMMUNICATIONS AUDIT

Now that you know what you want to achieve, you can begin to think about how you are going to achieve it. Your goal looms large before you and you are ready to begin developing a plan to reach it. Your next step is to think about your goal and other public relations efforts that you have conducted. What worked? What didn't work? An audit can help take the guesswork out of your public relations/communications planning. Just as the financial records kept by your library's accounting department are audited on a regular basis, it is important to audit your communications efforts and carefully evaluate your past efforts before investing time, energy, and money in another public relations cam-

---

FIGURE 2.2   Formulating a Public Relations/Communications Goal: University Library

1. What is it that you want to tell people?

   We want to tell people that our university's library is now open 24 hours.

2. Who do you want to tell?

   Students and faculty members

3. When do you want to communicate your message?

   September 1997—the beginning of the academic year and the kick-off of the new hours

4. Why do you want to tell people about this? Do you want them to do anything?

   We want to tell students and faculty members so they will take advantage of these hours and know that their university library is there to serve their needs. Also, we want to increase our gate count by 15 percent to justify the new hours.

Goal: Create faculty and student awareness of the university library's expanded hours by launching a multidimensional public relations campaign. Achieve a 15 percent increase in the library's overall gate count by the end of academic year 1997.

---

paign. An audit will help you determine what you are doing well and what you need to improve. It will also help you decide what communications tools have worked best for you in the past and what might be effective in the future. An audit will also provide you with a benchmark against which you can measure future communications efforts. You will know where you started when you developed your plan.

Communications audits measure perceptions of your organization by your key audiences. They can involve different types of research including focus groups and surveys. Begin by determining what audience you want to assess. For example, a university library conducting a communications audit might want to measure the perceptions of university faculty, staff, and students. Or, if one of the library's communications goals is to reach an audience beyond the university campus, it might be important to measure the perceptions of a particular group of community members, such as parents of school-age children, or a cross section of the entire community.

The next step is to determine how you currently communicate

FIGURE 2.3 Formulating a Public Relations/Communications Goal: Public Library

1. What is it that you want to tell people?
   We want to make people aware of the public library's programs and services.

2. Who do you want to tell?
   Community members

3. When do you want to communicate your message?
   1997

4. Why do you want to tell people about this? Do you want them to do anything?
   Circulation and gate counts are down. We need to increase both and promote the library's role in the community or our funding will be cut.

Goal: Increase public awareness of library services and programs by developing and implementing a year-long comprehensive public relations plan. Achieve a 15 percent increase in circulation and a 20 percent increase in gate count.

---

with this audience. A comprehensive list of all communications tools should be made. This list might include newsletters, brochures, flyers, mailings, news releases, electronic communication, signage, cable television programming, community presentations, and programming.

Based on your defined audience, the perception that you want to measure, and the communications tools that you have employed in the past, you can develop a research instrument for your audit. Then you are ready to assess the effectiveness of these efforts with your defined audience, and to find out how the audience perceives your organization and where that perception comes from.

If you are about to undertake a major public relations effort, you may wish to hire a public relations or communications firm to conduct an audit of your past communications efforts. The cost can run anywhere from $10,000 to $250,000 for a comprehensive communications audit.

If the idea of a formal audit by an impartial party appeals to you but far exceeds your financial limitations, you may want to approach a professor of communications at a local college or university. An upper-level or graduate student might be interested in evaluating your efforts as a special project or independent study.

There might still be some expenses, but you would save the consulting fees charged by a private firm and offer the student a valuable opportunity.

CONDUCTING YOUR OWN COMMUNICATIONS AUDIT

If an outside communications audit would consume your entire public relations budget, or if you are preparing a short-term, project-oriented public relations/communications plan, you can use some simple techniques to assess your past public relations efforts and determine what might work in the future. You can conduct an informal audit yourself by carefully and critically examining your past efforts.

A little bit of research into the current perceptions of your services and resources can provide you with a lot of information to use in your communications planning. By gathering information from users and nonusers, you can conduct a simple audit of your communications efforts and learn what information you are communicating effectively, what you need to communicate, and what misperceptions you might want to work to change.

Focus Groups

One way to gather information is to hold several small focus groups. A focus group is basically a guided group discussion. You gather a group of people who are willing to discuss the topic (such as library services in your community) and a facilitator leads them through a discussion of that topic. In the for-profit sector, focus group participants are usually paid a small fee for participating. It may not be possible or necessary for your library to pay individuals to spend one or two hours discussing your services; however, you should provide refreshments and be sure to follow up by sending a thank-you note to each participant.

Host both user and nonuser groups. The success of a focus group is dependent on the careful selection of the participants and the skills of the facilitator. Focus groups should never exceed about 10 participants and it is often helpful to have a neutral party—not a library employee—facilitate the session. Work with the facilitator to develop several leading questions for the participants and then let participants discuss their perceptions. The same questions should be asked at each focus group meeting so that results are comparable. You might begin a public library focus group with a question such as "What is the most valuable service this library provides and why?" Or you might start a focus group of students who are nonusers of a college library by asking them to "Name one reason that you don't use the library and tell us what we could do to change it."

You will want a record of the discussion at your focus group meetings. You might have a staff person attend and summarize on a flip chart the high points of the discussion, or, if the equipment is available, you might make an audio recording of the meeting.

The results of the focus groups will tell you where your strengths are, what needs to be changed, and, most importantly for your communications efforts, what areas of service and resources are not valued or viewed in the proper way by your constituents. By carefully examining those services, you may discover that nothing is wrong with the services—you just need to communicate the value of the services more clearly and positively.

Surveys

Another way to gather information is by survey. A short questionnaire asking participants to describe their perceptions of current services and materials or what services and materials they would like to see in the future can provide you with the background to plan your upcoming communications efforts. For example, you might ask whether or not you should provide access to the Internet in your branch libraries. If you have the time and resources to conduct both focus groups and a survey, you can use the findings from your focus groups to develop questions for your survey.

The key to surveying is to keep it short and simple. Personal interviews are an excellent way to get information. You can stop library users when they come into the library and ask them if they have a minute to answer a few questions. People like to share their opinions and are typically pleased when someone asks them thoughtful questions and listens to them. If you are trying to survey a limited number of people in a small environment, such as a school, you might simply want to distribute the questionnaire and ask participants to complete and return it. Under these circumstances the questionnaire must be easy to complete and easy to return, and it should ask about something that the audience cares about (for example, teachers would probably respond readily to a questionnaire asking about curriculum resources in the library).

Once you have done your simple research, examine the results thoughtfully. Determine the most important message to be communicated by the library and the most effective way to communicate it. Decide if you are going to develop an overall public relations/communications plan for the library or one focused only on a specific area or service.

DEVELOPING A PUBLIC RELATIONS/ COMMUNICATIONS PLAN

When you begin to develop a public relations/communications plan, it is best to start from scratch using the results of your research. If you have been producing a newsletter for years and the results of your audit show that it is an effective communications tool, keep it. Perhaps your research provided some suggestions for improving the newsletter. If so, apply them and you may end up with an even more effective communications tool.

A public relations/communications plan can have a very focused goal (such as to promote use of the library's video collection to children at East Township Branch), or a very broad goal (such as to communicate effectively to the community the services and programs of East Township City Libraries). You may determine this goal as a result of something you learned from your research. For example, perhaps you discovered that the children you interviewed don't even know you have a video collection and think you should add one—you may want to inform children about your collection. Or your communications goal may be determined by other factors. For instance, your library board may want to increase circulation or program attendance statistics, or your building principal may think that parents need to know more about the important role school libraries play in education.

A thoughtfully developed public relations/communications plan will be a road map for your efforts over the time period it addresses, and it will provide you with a way to measure the success of your work. If you use the information obtained in your research as you develop each objective and activity, your public relations/communications plan will likely lead you to your goal.

The major components of a public relations/communications plan are goals, objectives, and activities. You have already worked to define your goal earlier in this chapter. That goal should be the guiding force behind the development of all your objectives and activities. As you determine objectives for the plan, you need to ask, "What relationship does this objective have to our goal? Will it help us to achieve that goal?" Every objective should be clearly stated and measurable, with a clear time frame. If your objective is "to promote circulation," you would have no way of knowing if you were successful or not. On the other hand, if your objective is to increase circulation at your branch library by 5 percent in the next 12 months, that is measurable and you can develop communications activities to support that objective.

When writing objectives, it helps to state them as a verb in the infinitive form. For example, "To place three stories about the library's video collection in the local media during March, April, and May 1997" would be an objective. Activities are the steps that you will take to achieve each objective. "Develop press kits for the library's video collection and distribute them to all local media outlets" might be an activity to support the above objective. Identifying the primary person responsible for completing each activity will be critical to the success of your plan. The tasks outlined will then be clearly delegated and people will be more likely to complete the necessary tasks when they understand the expectations and can see them in relationship to the overall goal.

An outline for a public relations/communications plan and two sample plans based on the goals determined earlier in this chapter appear in the Appendix. In the outline, each component is briefly described. The sample plans provide an idea of what a public relations/communications plan for your library might look like. Other activities could be substituted for those presented or other supporting activities could be added. Both sample plans are project-based rather than comprehensive.

Remember that your public relations/communications plan is always a work in progress. Revisit it on a regular basis and assess where you are going. You may want to change directions or you may decide that you were too ambitious and want to pare it back a bit. Use it as a road map and refer to it often, but remember that you can always take a different route to achieve your goal.

Chapter 3 deals in-depth with two important components of communications planning—message development and determining your audience—and the chapters that follow provide information about strategies and tools that you may wish to use to communicate your message.

3 DEFINING YOUR LIBRARY'S MESSAGE AND AUDIENCE

The two important building blocks for your public relations/communications plan are message and audience. Effective public relations activities communicate a clear, consistent message to a carefully selected target audience. The message is reflected in reality, and the methods used to communicate it are appropriate for the audience you want to reach. Your public relations/communications efforts will be more successful if you spend extra time in your planning process thinking about the specific message you want to communicate and the audience you want to receive it. In addition, once you focus your message and determine your audience, the strategies and tools for your communications plan will begin to become apparent to you.

Wanting to tell everyone in your community that your library is good and they should use it is an admirable goal. But how do you go about communicating that message? Would time and resources allow you to reach everybody? What outcome do you want? Narrow that goal to increasing library use by parents of students enrolled in the local public schools. Focus your message on telling them how you can provide resources and activities for them and their children. Once you have a more manageable message, specific communications activities, such as having your branch libraries set up information booths at school parent nights, will begin to emerge as possible ways of communicating your message and accomplishing the goal.

Message and audience are the two components of your public relations/communications plan that should be pretty much set in stone once your plan is developed. You may want to change your strategies or approach or make your goal more manageable, but once you determine what you want to say and who you want to say it to, staying the course is the best bet for achieving your goal (unless, of course, you discover that you have not chosen the right audience or that your message doesn't reflect the reality of your situation). By reading the rest of this chapter and thoughtfully answering the questions about your message and your audience, you should be able to develop a message and target audience early in your planning process and then work toward strategies for getting the word out.

DEVELOPING YOUR MESSAGE

A clear, consistent message is key to the success of your communications efforts. After you answer the question, "What is it that you want to tell people?" and even after you develop your public relations/communications plan, you will want to spend time developing and refining your message. It cannot be ambiguous and you must work to ensure that all of your materials carry the same message, if not the same words. Ambiguity is created and mixed messages are communicated when your message is not consistent with reality.

Your message should also be focused. Don't try to tell people everything at once or in one communications effort. If you are simply trying to change perceptions, then your message should communicate whatever the perception is that you are trying to create. But, if the aim of your message is to get people to act, then make sure your message tells them what you want them to do. If you want them to check out more books, communicate that action: "Anytown Public Library—Check Us Out!" If you want people to think your library is a safe place, develop a message that says "Anytown Public Library—A Safe Place." Don't let clever words and slogans get in the way of your message. It is better to be clear and get the word out than to be clever and confuse a lot of people.

LIBRARY POLICIES, PROCEDURES, AND ENVIRONMENT AND YOUR MESSAGE

Not only does your message need to be clear and consistent; it also needs to reflect the reality of your library's policies, procedures, and environment. Don't try to tell the public one thing about your library when your practice tells them something completely different.

For example, if you want people to think of your public library as a community center, you need to look at all of your library's public relations materials and make sure that they convey that message. In addition, you may need to examine library policies and procedures to be sure that they reflect that message. Library policies and practices cannot contradict your message. If they do you need either to change the policies or change the message. For instance, you can't try to convince the public that your library is a center for the community if your meeting rooms are locked at 6 p.m. every day and unavailable for community group meetings. A policy change will be necessary before you can effectively communicate the message that the library is a community center.

Your message must also be reflected in the staff's attitude and behavior. For example, if you are trying to encourage neighbors from the area surrounding your university library to use your services and resources, but staff give a look that says, "Who are you and what are you doing here?' to everyone who doesn't appear to be a student or a faculty member, your message is contradicted by staff behavior. Part of your communications plan must include working with the library staff to convince them of the importance of a good relationship with university neighbors. In addition, a new library policy about providing service to nonuniversity patrons might need to be established and implemented. Communicating a message that isn't reflected in policy and practice is misleading, damaging to your credibility, and ultimately a waste of your effort.

The perception you are trying to create and the message you are trying to communicate must also be reflected in the library's environment. For example, an elementary school library media specialist who has just purchased a collection of parenting materials and is trying to encourage adults from the neighborhood to visit the library and use the collection should provide chairs that are comfortable for adults in addition to the little chairs designed for the regular patrons. Perhaps the parenting collection should be set to one side in the library so that parents can come in unobtrusively and use the materials out of the student traffic and commotion. The collection needs to be on a shelf that is a good height for adults and labeled clearly. Parents, who come in response to the flyer inviting them to visit the school library to use the collection, will see an environment that reflects the message presented in words on the flyer.

Another example is a public library that wants to encourage teenagers to use its services. Lots of wonderful, teen-appropriate promotional materials are designed and distributed through the schools and other youth organizations. Yet, when the teens arrive at the library, they find their area is a corner of the children's room and the furniture is about the right size for fifth graders. In addition, the materials in the young adult collection aren't age appropriate and they are battered and worn. The promotional materials communicate one message and the environment—the reality—reflects another.

Another public library received a grant to have its cardholder information translated into several Asian languages, such as Vietnamese and Laotian. Translation was costly, but it was done and the materials were made available in the different languages. News releases were sent out announcing that cardholder materials were now available in languages for new immigrants. When a reporter arrived to do a story, however, the real story was that, while the library had registration materials in Vietnamese and Laotian, there were no materials in the library's collection in those languages. Registration materials were geared to welcome new users, but the collection did not provide them with any resources.

The bottom line is: If you don't have it, don't try to sell it! Developing a message that is inconsistent with your library's policy or environment sends your audience a mixed message and leaves them confused and doubtful about your library and its credibility.

VISUALS AND YOUR MESSAGE

You will probably use some type of artwork—perhaps photographs, drawings, or graphic designs—to tell your story. Again, your visuals must reflect your message. If you want teens to think the library is a place where they should hang out, don't send them a brochure featuring pictures of preschoolers or senior citizens. Send them a brochure with pictures of teenagers in the library.

In the example of the parent collection in the school library media center, the flyer sent to parents needs to be designed for parents, not children. Cute teddy bears might not be the best artwork to promote a serious collection of materials that will help your students' parents develop their parenting skills.

Remember that, if you want your library to be perceived as a friendly place, the people featured in any drawings or photographs you use should be smiling and look friendly. Be sure that drawings and photographs reflect cultural diversity and include both genders. It is important for people to be able to identify with the people they see in your artwork. For example, if the words on your brochure say "Anytown Public Library Is a Great Place for Senior Citizens," a photograph of an older African American female patron smiling and working with a library staff person will reinforce your message. On the other hand, a 45–year-old frowning woman sitting alone at a reading table doesn't do much to tell your story. Visuals should complement and enhance your message, not detract from or contradict it.

BUDGET AND YOUR MESSAGE

Quality communications materials will be important to the success of your efforts. "Quality," however, does not necessarily mean "expensive." Pay close attention to what you are spending on communications materials, particularly if your message has any budget connotations.

For example, if you are launching a campaign to encourage the community to pass an operating levy for your library and your message is "Anytown Public Library: The Best Bargain in

Town," developing and distributing four-color brochures might not be the best way to spread the word. A simple, one-color piece will be effective and speaks loudly itself. It says, "Anytown Public Library Does Quality, Cost-Effective Work."

A public library once published a "wish catalog" of items it wanted people to consider donating money for to the library. This catalog was elegant, with photographs, expensive paper, and three colors of ink. Library patrons complained that the money spent printing the catalog could have been used to purchase several of the items the library was "wishing" for. While the catalog was a beautiful printed piece and even won national awards, its extravagance was inconsistent with the library's message—"We Need Donations."

CREDIBILITY AND YOUR MESSAGE

If you promise people something, be sure you do it! Asking people to donate money to your library's "Buy a Book" program and promising that, for each $25 they donate, their name will appear on a bookplate in a book in your collection may be a great idea. But, be sure that you follow through—so that when Mr. Jones shows up to see the three books that his $75 bought, you can show them to him. If you don't follow through you destroy your credibility—the next time you try to communicate with Mr. Jones he will be skeptical. It is better not to promise an outcome than to promise one and not follow through on it.

An example of damaged credibility is a public library that conducted a bond issue campaign for new buildings. A charming photograph of two library patrons using bookmobile services was included in the informational materials. The words in the materials did not state that bookmobile services would be continued after the bond issue passed, but the photograph's inclusion in the bond issue informational materials implied that to many community members. The library's credibility suffered significant damage when, three months after the bond issue passed, bookmobile services were discontinued. There may or may not have been a plan to stop running the bookmobile at the time that the bond issue materials were developed. But, some community members viewed using the photograph in the materials as a blatant way of manipulating bookmobile patrons into voting for the bond issue.

Library suggestion boxes provide another excellent example of making sure your message is consistent with your actions. For example, a library has a suggestion box for patrons with a sign that says, "When you talk, we listen." Patrons who complete the suggestion form, put it in the box, but never see any responses posted or mailed to them are shown that "When you talk, we don't care." Such a library would be better off without a mechanism for patron suggestions, than to have one to which it isn't responsive.

THE MEDIA AND YOUR MESSAGE

Always make sure reality is consistent with your message when dealing with the media. Don't make an exception to a policy for a reporter or change practice to provide him with assistance unless you want to see it on the six o'clock news. If a reporter asks for access to your patron database, don't provide it and tell him it will be your "little secret." The same policies apply to the press as apply to the general public.

You can, however, work to ensure that when a reporter comes to cover a story, you present the story in the best possible light. An example of this would be writing and sending out a news release that talks about your successful summer reading program and how your libraries are constantly full of children. You get a call from a television reporter who wants to come that afternoon and do a story based on this release. This is a great opportunity. Obviously, choose a time when you know for sure children will be in the library. You may want to make an announcement during story hour that a television reporter will be doing a story on your summer reading program on Wednesday at 3:00 p.m. Watch how many kids turn out! Don't risk telling a different story by having the reporter show up at the Main Library and there not being any children around.

CONSISTENT, NOT COMPLICATED

All of these warnings about making sure that your message reflects reality and isn't contradicted by your library's practice may seem to make telling your library's story terribly complicated. It really isn't. You can develop a clear, simple message, be sure that it isn't contradicted by reality, communicate it clearly and consistently, and implement an extremely successful public relations/communications plan. Common sense and good judgment are the only skills that you need to develop a message that will tell the community what your library is really all about.

Once you decide what your message is going to be—what it is that you want to tell people and possibly ask them to do—then ask the following questions:

1. Are we currently doing everything we are talking about?
2. Are we telling the complete truth?
3. Do any of our policies, procedures, or practices contradict this message?

4. If we are promising something, can we follow through?
5. Does our environment reflect what our message is saying?
6. Would I believe this message if I heard it? Would I act in the way that I am being asked to act? Why or why not?

Your answers to these questions will help you to more clearly define your message. If there are conflicts, you can either decide to change your message to reflect reality or change reality to reflect your message. It is a good idea to convene a mini-focus group of library employees to evaluate your message based on these questions. You will find the different perspectives, particularly from those who weren't involved in the development of your message, very helpful as you determine whether or not you need to make changes.

The most important question to consider is number six, Would I believe this message if I heard it? Would I act in the way that I am being asked to act? Why or why not? If your message doesn't seem consistent with reality to you or to other library staff, then you cannot expect to convince an external audience that it is true or to act on it. The responses to this question may tell you to completely start over in terms of developing a message or may tell you that you are on the right track and provide you with information that will be helpful as you develop strategies for communicating your message.

TARGETING YOUR AUDIENCE

Deciding "who" you want to communicate with is equally important as deciding "what" you want to say. Answering the question, "Who do we want to tell?" may seem simple. However, choosing your target audience(s) is essential to the success of your public relations/communications efforts and should be given thoughtful consideration. You can develop a clear, consistent message that reflects reality, and a wonderful public relations/communications plan with great strategies and implement that plan without a hitch. But if you aren't communicating your message to the right audience(s), it will all be for naught. If you want to pass a bond issue, you can't waste time and energy telling your story to teenagers who can't vote or to citizens from another county. When time and resources are limited, it is important to carefully target your audience(s) and then work hard to get your message out to that audience(s).

Choosing an audience(s) is much easier when you have a project-based message. If you are working on promoting preschool storytime, then parents of preschoolers are your obvious audience. As a university library trying to increase gate count, your obvious audience is students and faculty members. However, you might want to consider focusing on community members instead, depending upon your overall communications goals.

Even when you have a message that needs to be communicated to a wide audience(s), it might be better to focus on one segment of that audience(s) at a time. A school library media specialist's overall communications goal might be to convince the faculty in her school that Internet resources can contribute to the curriculum. However, she might decide that for the first three months, the audience that she is going to target will be third grade science teachers. She will focus more energy on that audience for a short period of time.

The bottom line is the "scattershot" approach to communications does not work. You can't just develop your message, send it out there, and hope someone receives it. The whole purpose of developing a public relations/communications plan is to ensure that you make careful decisions about what your message is, how you communicate it, and to whom you communicate it. Any marksman knows you don't accomplish anything if you just close your eyes, fire your gun, and hope for the best. You need to aim it at a target. The same goes for your library's communications efforts: If you aim, you have a better chance of hitting the target.

Carefully selecting target audiences for your message will help you to choose strategies and tools for communicating it. If your target audience is senior citizens, the local rock radio station is probably not the best media outlet for you to work with on communicating this message. And if you choose to get your message across via a newsletter, you might want to consider using large print.

Targeting an audience or audiences will help you to spend your limited human and fiscal resources in the most effective way. It gives you a focus for your efforts.

HOW TO CHOOSE YOUR AUDIENCE

Libraries and librarians have a tendency to want to be all things to all people. So, choosing target audiences may not come naturally to most librarians. While it would be nice to be able to tell everything to everybody, time and resource constraints don't make that practical.

Before selecting the target audience for your particular message, however, it is a good exercise to brainstorm a list of your library's possible audiences. List them under two headings—internal and external. An internal audience is an audience within your organization. Further, it is an audience that you will need to help you to communicate your message. An external audience is an audience outside your organization that you want to reach with your message. For a public library, internal audiences might include staff, library board members, friends of the library, and volunteers. A school library might include teachers, the principal, other school staff, and volunteers as its internal audiences. External audiences for a public library would be community members, city council members, state and federal legislators, the national library community, and more. Friends of the library and volunteers could also be on a public library's list of external audiences. A school library's external audiences might be the community, school board, parents, and students.

Confusing? Definitely. Unfortunately, defining your audience is not a cut-and-dried activity. Like developing your message, determining your target audience(s) is a judgment call. Once you brainstorm the list of possible audiences, think about them in terms of the message and answer the following questions:

1. Who is the message geared toward? Is it geared toward them as an internal or an external audience?
2. How much time do you have to communicate this message?
3. Do you need action on this? If so, who is capable of acting?

First, think carefully about who your message is really for. Are you talking to adults or children? Are you working to convince policy makers or the general public? You can't afford to spend time telling the story to people you don't necessarily need to reach.

Second, the amount of time that you have to communicate your message will also help you to select your target audience(s). For example, if you have years and a very broad message, you might want a very broad target audience—perhaps community members, from infants to age 90. You can then develop a plan with objectives that target the different age groups.

The third question should really help you to narrow your focus. Is this a message that requires action? If so, who can act? Promoting preschool storytime to increase attendance by sending flyers to senior citizens in nursing homes doesn't make much sense. However, sending flyers home to parents with children from local preschools does make sense. Answering this question honestly will help you focus your efforts on the audience who can most help you achieve your goal.

After answering the questions, you should have a narrower list of audiences for this particular message. Consider audiences carefully. Is it realistic to target all of them, considering the time and resources available? If the answer is yes, move onward. If it is no, would it be better to do a more comprehensive job of telling your story with a smaller target audience? Or perhaps some audiences should be "major" targets for your plan while others should be "minor." (Major targets would be the focus of most of your efforts; activities would address the minor target audience, but they wouldn't be the focus of your plan.)

THE IMPORTANCE OF INTERNAL AUDIENCES

When you are developing your plan and considering your target audience(s), give serious thought to your internal audiences. The library staff is the best communications tool available to you. What a circulation clerk says over his back fence about your library will have much greater impact than any flyer or slick brochure that you produce. Convening a staff advisory committee for your communications efforts and including staff at all levels in the decision-making process is a great way to ensure buy-in for your efforts. At times, however, such a committee isn't advisable or practical. In those cases, at the very least, make sure that staff receive information before it is distributed to the public. In addition give staff the same time and consideration for questions about an issue that you would give to a reporter from the local television station. Your efforts are guaranteed to pay off and be reflected in staff attitudes toward you and your efforts.

Above all, never, ever, overlook your internal audience. It is critical to the success of your external communications. Before you launch any type of campaign or public relations effort, be sure that your internal audience is working for you. Provide them with clear, consistent information and take their ideas and suggestions under careful consideration. Remember that they are on the front lines dealing with the public. They hear the concerns, comments, and perceptions of the public on a daily basis. The information and insight that they have will be invaluable to you as you develop and implement your public relations/communications plan.

"WHO" DETERMINES HOW

Once you have identified your target audience(s), you will be ready to think about how you want to communicate with them. If you are looking at using print or broadcast media, the demographics of the various media outlets will help you decide which ones to target. The age and ability levels of your audiences will help you decide what type of approach to take to communicate your message, what your print and graphic design should look like, and what types of special activities might help to tell your story.

For example, if a primary target audience is the new readers involved in your library's literacy program, you will want to ensure that materials are written on a level they can understand. If you want to reach senior citizens you will need to pay special attention to typeface size. If your target is school-age children, it is easy to reach them through school. The list of possible communications tools and strategies begins to develop once you have defined your target audiences.

CONCLUSION

Determining your public relations/communications message and selecting target audiences for that message is hard work, but it is the first important step toward meeting your communications goal. Once you have established "what" you want to say and "who" you want to say it to, you will be able to determine "what" are the best tools for reaching your audience. This is the part of public relations work that is really fun. Selecting and developing your communications tools are opportunities to use your creativity and to work directly with a wide variety of people in your community.

In the chapters that follow, various communications tools and strategies will be described and approaches for using them will be discussed. As you consider how you will communicate your message, always remember to consider your audience(s) carefully. Think about each tool or strategy in terms of "Will this work with teenagers? senior citizens? parents of preschoolers? teachers? students? faculty members?" By building on each component in your public relations/communications plan, you will develop an approach that is geared to your audience(s) and that aims your message directly at your target audience(s).

4 DEVELOPING A CORPORATE IDENTITY FOR YOUR LIBRARY

In his recent book *The Pursuit of Wow!* Tom Peters details a variety of reasons for considering the design or the "look" of your communications materials. While Peters is addressing primarily a corporate audience, all of his 142 definitions of design can be applied to libraries and should be thought-provoking as you consider developing a graphic corporate image for your library.[1]

Whether you are managing communications efforts for a large public library system or a library media center in a small elementary school, you will want to develop a graphic corporate identity for your library. That identity and the style elements that accompany it will serve as a guide as you develop all of your communications materials, including print and electronic materials, bookplates, signage, and identification stickers on your library van.

By developing a graphic identity or look for your library, you will be working to create a particular public perception of your library. For example, if you want to be perceived as an all-business corporate library, you will want the colors and design of your corporate identity to be conservative. You might use white paper and have your corporate colors be blue and gray. If you are a creating an identity for your academic library, but you want students to think it is a fun place, you might choose brighter colors and a more casual style for your materials.

THE IMPORTANCE OF DESIGN

Even before you decide that you want to develop printed communications materials for your library, you will want to begin thinking about design. The corporate graphic image that you develop will guide you in designing communications materials to meet your public relations goal. Someone who looks at a brochure produced by your library should immediately recognize that it is yours before reading any of the information. Occasionally, you will want to create unique materials that stray from the dictates of your library's corporate style in order to attract special attention. For example, if you are trying to attract teenagers to your public library, you may want to use a flyer that doesn't look like it came from a library. But, in general, you will want to establish a look for your library and stick with that look for all of your printed materials and electronic promotion materials (such as a Web Page) and for your library's stationery. Think about the corporate identities of companies such as Nike, McDonald's, or Coke. They may have different advertising campaigns and their materials may have slightly different looks, but, you always know immediately who the ad comes from. A mixture of looks, colors, and paper types for your library's printed materials not only makes your literature racks unattractive, it also projects an image of a cluttered organization that doesn't know where it is going.

When you design your print materials or any item for your library, think about the different types of design that are out there. In his list Peters includes examples of the simplicity of design, the eclectic nature of design, and the importance of design. His diverse list (which even includes bad examples of design) emphasizes the importance of developing a look—a design—that belongs exclusively to your library.

DEVELOPING YOUR CORPORATE IDENTITY

Your library's corporate identity will be the foundation on which much of your communications efforts will be built. Since it will be featured in most of your communications materials, you might want to hire an outside graphic design or public relations firm to assist you. Design firms charge anywhere from $500 to $5,000 to develop the type of corporate identity package that a public library might want. Perhaps a local design firm will be willing to do pro bono or reduced fee work for your library. Just ask! Lots of people have warm feelings about what libraries have done for them and would welcome the opportunity to repay the library.

If you can't afford an outside design firm, there may be a student at a local art or design school who would be willing to develop your library's corporate identity as a class project. A talented friend of the library or staff member might be willing to volunteer.

Academic and school libraries, as with other parts of their communications efforts, may want to work with their parent institutions' communications offices to develop an identity that complements the organization's overall identity. A simple addition to the parent institution's materials, such as an icon attached to the logo or an additional color, would create an identity for a school or academic library that is distinctive but also consistent with the overall image of their organization.

Whether you are working with a volunteer or a paid design firm, it is important to start your process with a written agreement about what will be developed and on what timeline, how many times the artwork will be reviewed and by whom, and how many times the alterations will be made. This agreement will guide your progress and will prevent any misunderstandings.

An overall corporate identity package might include

- logo
- corporate colors
- stylesheet for different uses of the logo and colors
- corporate typestyle
- stationery
- newsletter template (optional)
- brochure template (optional)
- program flyer template (optional)
- signage template (optional)

Be very specific with the designer about what you are trying to achieve and what you can afford to spend on your communications materials both now and in the future. You may have $5,000 to invest in the development of the corporate identity package, but if you can't afford to print the stationery they design, then it's not the right design for your library.

From the beginning of the process, be sure that the designer meets with the key decision-makers for your library. If your library director will have the final approval on the design, then the designer must meet with the director early in the process. The designer will ask the director questions about the image that he or she wants to project and may review some other corporate identity packages to get a sense of the director's taste. When you meet with the designer on your own, you may want to share other pertinent information, such as "Our library director hates pink." The major question to answer throughout this process is "What image does this library want to project and will these materials help us to do that?"

During the design process, you will want to show the logo designs and colors to a variety of people for their reactions. This is a good way to find out how the public will react. It is best, however, that the final approval decision not be made by a committee or the library board. Design is a very personal matter, and it is hard for a group to agree on a design because they tend to think about it in terms of their personal likes rather than what will get the job done. Some designers may even charge more if they know that the decision is made by a committee or board, rather than one or two individuals because they believe the work process will be more cumbersome.

CHOOSING A DESIGNER

If you decide to work with a design firm to develop your library's corporate identity, be sure to select someone who will work well with you and your library. Looking in the yellow pages under "graphic designers" is one strategy. Also, larger communities may have special directories of designers, including more information about each firm and samples of their work. Word of mouth may be the best way to find a good designer, however. Look at the communications materials of other organizations in your community. When you find something you like, call the organization's communications director and ask who did the design. People are usually pleased to make referrals to firms especially when they are happy with the work. Another great source for referrals to designers is the people who sell printing or paper to your library. They often work directly with designers and know a lot about firms in your community.

Once you get some referrals, call the designers and tell them about your project. If the firm is interested, ask them to send you a few samples of their work. If you like what they send, call them back and schedule a meeting to discuss your project. Ask the designer to bring a portfolio to your meeting so that you can see the variety of work that the designer has done. You may also want to visit the designer's studio to get a sense of the atmosphere and work environment. After you find two or three firms that might be appropriate to design your library's corporate identity, ask each to provide a proposal and quote based on the job that you describe. Compare the quotes and make your decision. If your policy doesn't dictate that you go with the lowest bidder, be sure to consider how you feel about the designers. If all three designers quote the same fee, but you seem to "click" with one of them, hire that one! Design is an extremely intuitive process and it is important to trust your intuition when hiring a designer.

WORKING WITH A DESIGNER

Don't worry if you have never worked with a designer before and know nothing about graphic design. Operate under the maxim, "I don't know much about art, but I know what I like." Show the proposed designs to others and remember to voice your opinion when you don't like something even if you aren't sure why. On the other hand, trust the designer you hire as the expert. If you don't like something, express your opinion, but rely on the designer to correct the problem. Don't spend your time trying to change or redesign the logo yourself. If it becomes apparent that this designer really isn't producing ideas that will work for your library, talk to the designer. There might be someone else in the firm who can take over your account or the designer might recommend that you find another firm that can better meet your library's needs.

BUILDING THE PACKAGE

Once you have selected the designer for your library's corporate identity, it is time to begin building the package. The designer will want to work closely with you on each stage of development so that the materials meet your library's communications needs. Each element in the package builds on the next. The first decisions you make will be about a logo, colors, and stationery.

LOGOS

Working with a designer to develop a logo for your library is a chance to design one graphic image that represents what your library is all about. A good logo should be simple and eye-catching, and reproduce as well in black and white as it does in color. The complete name of the organization should be integrated into the artwork.

You may want your library's logo to include something representative of your community. If it already does and you also want to use it to communicate to people outside of your community, such as libraries around the country, ask some people who don't live in your community for their opinion of it. If they can't tell what it is, then you might want to change the logo. *Print* magazine publishes an annual issue of logos from around the world including library logos. You may want to look at some back issues before you begin your logo design process.

If your library already has a logo but it is dated, you may wish to have the designer update it rather than start from scratch. This is an especially good strategy if the current logo is well known and your library has a good reputation. By simply updating your current logo, you are using it to communicate the message, "Our library isn't changing, it is simply moving into the 21st century."

Stylesheet for Use of Logo

Developing a stylesheet for the use of your library's logo is important to maintaining the integrity of your corporate identity. This stylesheet will provide you and other library staff with guidelines for how and when to use the logo. If it is a three-color logo, the stylesheet can specify how the logo should be used in a two-color application, a one-color application, or black ink only. It will describe how the logo should be reduced and enlarged, where it should be placed on materials, and how it can or cannot be altered. The guidelines provided by the stylesheet will help to ensure the consistency of your library's graphic images. Copies of the stylesheet should be distributed to anyone who might use the logo on any materials.

CORPORATE TYPESTYLE

A specific type font will be used for the copy included in your logo. It may be a standard font or a font that is specially altered for your use. In addition, your designer will want to determine one or two fonts for use in all of your communications materials. The designer will determine what sizes and styles of font (bold, italics, reverse) you should use and when. This information will be included on your stylesheet. By following these guidelines, you will produce materials that have a "family" look instead of looking cluttered or messy.

Stationery

When people receive a letter from your library, the very first impression that they get will be from your letterhead. You will want it to have a design that communicates your desired perception of your library. If you want people to perceive your library as a dignified research institution, your letterhead should have a very corporate look. If your message is that the library is a fun and exciting place, your letterhead should reflect that image. The point is be sure that your colors and paper type reflect, and don't detract from, your image. The list of colors in Figure 4.1 and what they mean to most people will help you work with your designers to select proper colors for your library. Once you select those colors, they will be the corporate colors for your organization and should be used on many of your materials, including business cards, brochures, newsletters, and signage.

FIGURE 4.1 Color as a Symbol

Color can create a mood, symbolize ideas, and provoke emotions. Your library's colors should be carefully selected based on the image you want to project. Consider the following impacts of colors when making your selection:

Color	Idea/Emotion
• Red	happiness, excitement, bravery, danger
• Blue	dignity, serenity, loyalty, honesty
• Black	death
• Yellow	cowardice
• White	purity or innocence
• Purple	royalty or wealth
• Green	life or hope[2]

There are many wonderful kinds of paper to choose from for your letterhead. Be sure that you can afford the one you select. In addition, make sure that the paper will really meet your needs. Will it photocopy well? Will it work in the paper tray of your photocopier and go through your laser printer? It may be beautiful speckled paper, but do the speckles make the text printed on the paper hard to read? Remember that the look of your stationery is important, but it is a communications tool and the look shouldn't hinder communicating.

The design of your letterhead shouldn't get in the way of your message either. Some letterhead designs are graphically interesting but not very practical. If the designer presents you with letterhead that has printed information at both the top and the bottom of the page or in both the right and left margins there may not be much space left for the letter itself. Think carefully about how restrictive this type of design will be before choosing it.

Another consideration is the information that you want to include on your letterhead. Traditionally, you would include your library's name, address, and phone and fax numbers. Some libraries also print the name of the library director and/or library board members on their letterhead. This is a nice touch, but can get expensive since your letterhead becomes obsolete with every name change. You might also include your library's e-mail and web page addresses if you have them. If you put all of this information on your letterhead, it will be informative, but making it not look cluttered may be a challenge to the designer. Consider carefully what is the most important information to include.

Templates

Particularly if you or other staff members are skilled at desktop publishing, you may want to have the designer develop a variety of templates for print materials using your library's corporate identity. Possibilities include templates for a newsletter, brochures, program flyers, or signage. The designer will provide you with a look for these items and you can "fill in the blanks" when the need for a brochure or flyer arises. The designer should develop a stylesheet for each type of template telling you what typestyle and sizes to use and detailing other design considerations. Using the template and the stylesheet, you will be able to create materials that support your library's public relations activities and reflect the organization's overall corporate identity.

INTRODUCING NEW MATERIALS

If your library already has a logo and supporting corporate identity materials, and you are updating or totally redoing your image, you will want to consider how to introduce your new materials. The best way to start using your new materials is to discard all the old items. But first be sure that you can afford to do that and that your timeline is long enough to have everything done on time. Later, you might have a special event to "unveil" your new logo and colors. You could hold a press conference or do this at an already scheduled event, such as a board meeting or parent's night at your school. Such an event is an opportunity for your library director or board president to talk about why these materials were developed, the image that your library is trying to project, and why.

CONCLUSION

Developing a corporate identity will be a first step in creating a positive public perception of your library. You will be able to design materials that communicate the image you want your library to project—and that design can pervade all of your communications materials. As Tom Peters says, "Design is at least as important for corporations grossing $250,000 a year as for those grossing $25 billion per year."[3] Design is as important for libraries with a $50,000 budget as for those with a $50 million budget.

NOTES

1. Tom Peters, *The Pursuit of WOW! Every Person's Guide to Topsy-Turvy Times* (New York: Random House, 1994), 120–127.
2. Robert O. Bone, Robert E. Sintons, and Philip R. Wigg, *Art Fundamentals: Theory and Practice* (Dubuque, Iowa: William C. Brown Co. Publishers, 1968), 95.
3. Peters, 122.

5 CREATING EFFECTIVE PRINT COMMUNICATIONS

This may be the age of technology and electronic communications, but in many cases, print materials are still the best way to communicate your message. They are particularly good for promoting special events and services. However, before you decide "We need a brochure for that" or "Let's do a newsletter," there are a variety of things you should think about. Considering whether or not print is the best medium for your message is especially important in light of the many electronic means of communications that are available today. Chapter 10 discusses using electronic resources, such as the Internet, to communicate with your audiences.

The reality is that, at least right now, most of the audiences that most libraries want to reach don't have access to electronic communications. Exceptions may be academic libraries at universities, where all students and faculty have e-mail addresses, and some corporations and government agencies. In most cases, if you decide to publish something on the World Wide Web or send it out as an e-mail bulletin, you probably will want to publish it in print also. In addition to the issue of access, we have not culturally adapted to the idea of electronic publication. For example, a library newsletter may include a calendar of events that people will want to post on their refrigerator or they may want to read it on the bus in the morning. Libraries should certainly pursue electronic promotion of their services and resources, but they must be sure that their audiences have equal access to that information. To do that, print is still the best option.

This chapter will take you through the process of planning, budgeting, and scheduling your library's publications. It will help you think about whether your printing and design can be done in-house or whether they should be contracted out. It also provides tips for working with printers and designers. If you would like step-by-step help with actually producing print publications, *Creating Newsletters, Brochures and Pamphlets: A How-to-Do-It Manual for School and Public Librarians*, (Neal-Schuman, 1992) by Barbara Radke Blake and Barbara L. Stein, is an excellent resource.

PUBLICATION PLANNING FOR YOUR LIBRARY

There are many options for print publications. You may want to produce a regular newsletter or intermittent promotional flyers. Your library may publish one overall service brochure or a separate brochure for each type of service. The goals and objectives that you detail in your public relations/communications plan should help you to make decisions about the type of print publications necessary to meet your overall communications goal.

EDITORIAL STYLE SHEET

Once you determine what items you need and can afford, you will want to develop an editorial stylesheet to guide the content development for any publication that your library produces. As part of the development of your library's corporate image, you have already developed a graphic stylesheet to guide the design of your publications. An editorial stylesheet will help ensure consistency within the content of your library's publications.

You may wish to adhere to one of several editorial style manuals, such as *The Chicago Manual of Style* or the *Associated Press Style Book*. This makes sense because such guides make many major editing decisions for you. You simply develop a list of editorial standards specific to your library in addition to those published in the manuals you choose to follow. The *Associated Press (AP) Style Book* is the easiest to use and the types of usage it recommends may be most familiar to your audiences since it is used by most major newspapers. It will help you and your authors decide when to use words or figures to represent numbers, agree on standard abbreviations for states, and decide when to capitalize certain words and titles.

You will, however, want to develop a customized stylesheet for your library. This special guide will include how you want to refer to your library in first and second reference. For example, all first references might be "Anytown Public Library" and second references might be "the Library." By determining the style for these references and publishing and distributing that information, you will help ensure consistency in all of your library's publications. This consistency will contribute to the quality of your overall image.

Developing an editorial stylesheet may take a bit of time, but it will be time well spent. You will find that it makes developing the content for any future publication a lot easier and provides any author in your library with guidelines for his or her writing. You may even want to recommend that the stylesheet be used to guide the writing of business letters and other corporate communications, in addition to actual publications. It will also be useful for electronic publishing.

PUBLICATION DESCRIPTION

You will want to develop a publication description for each item that you plan to publish. It should be based on the goals and objectives of your public relations/communications plan and ultimately will become a part of that plan. The development of this description also provides another opportunity for you to decide if the print publication you are considering meets your communications needs. You may get halfway through writing the description and discover that you already have a publication that meets the goal of your new publication. Or, after developing the description, you may compare it to your public relations/communications plan and decide that there is no relationship between the two—the new publication was a nice idea, but it wouldn't further your library's communications goal.

Above all, the publication description will be an important communication tool when you work with the publication's writers and designers. It will describe exactly what you want your new newsletter, brochure, or flyer to look like and the goals you want to achieve with it. See Figure 5.1 for an outline of a publication description. Figures 5.3 and 5.4 are sample outlines for a newsletter and a brochure, but the samples can be customized to suit any type of publication that you are considering.

BUDGETING FOR PUBLICATIONS

The information in your publication description will help you develop a draft budget for your publication. You can total the number of people in your audience, get some printing quotes, and determine how many of them you can realistically afford to reach. You may discover that while a four-color publication would be great, two ink colors are all that you can afford. Once you develop a budget based on this information and decide what you can truly afford, you should update the description to reflect what your publication will really be like. In addition, this information will provide you with a plan for developing the content for your publication and its printing and distribution.

Each publication that you produce should have its own budget and you should keep careful track of expenditures for that publication. This information will help you measure the effectiveness

FIGURE 5.1 Publication Description Outline

Purpose: What is the goal of this publication? What do you want to communicate or promote? Think about how it relates to your library's overall communications goal.

Description: This should be a physical description of the publication. What size are you thinking about? How many colors of ink would you like to use? Will it include photos?

Publication Dates: How often will this publication be published or revised? If it is a newsletter, include a publication schedule. If it is a brochure, you will probably want to include a revision schedule.

Audience: Provide a detailed list of your audience with a ballpark number of members of each group (for example, parents of school-age children in our community—10,000; all members of the friends of the library—2,000).

Number Produced: Based on your audience, how many copies of this item do you plan to print?

Cost: You may not be able to fill in this figure when first developing your description, but you can use the information that you put in this description to determine how much your publication will cost. When you have that information, provide it here both in terms of total cost and cost per item.

Content: What will the content of this publication be? How will it address the audience?

Distribution: Merely producing a print publication doesn't communicate anything to your audience. From the very beginning, you need to have a plan for distributing the publication to your target audience. You will have spent your money wisely if you know from the start who is going to get your publication and how. You would have been better off not publishing the item—even if it is spectacular in terms of content and design—if it just sits in boxes under a table in your library's workroom.

Person Responsible: As for every item in your public relations/communications plan, you will want to designate one person who is responsible for the publication. That person doesn't have to do all of the work, but he or she does have to coordinate it. That person is responsible for seeing that the publication is reviewed for revision on schedule, that the planned distribution occurs, and that it stays on its publication schedule.

of your communications efforts based on the resources that you have dedicated to them. It is just as important to keep track of the number of staff hours spent on the publication as the actual dollars that have been paid for design, printing, and distribution.

Basically, copywriting, design, photos or other artwork, printing, and distribution will be the basic elements in any publication budget. You'll need to determine which tasks will be done in-house and which will be done by outside professionals. Then you can begin to build a budget based on price quotes from outside professionals and your own estimates of the time for in-house work.

Copywriting

In many cases, you will probably decide to do at least the preliminary copywriting in-house. You and your staff are the closest to the topic and can pull the information together most quickly. You may, however, want to consider employing an outside editor to review your copy. This is particularly important when developing items that you expect to have a long life, such as service brochures. Many freelance copywriters work inexpensively ($20 and up per hour). They can edit your copy based on your style guide, correct any grammatical errors, and catch any professional jargon that might have found its way into your copy. In addition, they might be able to put a little "flavor" or "spin" into copy about a topic that you have become too close to.

Design

With the prevalence of easy desktop publishing programs and personal computers on many desks, you have many choices about how to manage the design of your publications. If you have a large budget, using an outside designer is your best choice. No matter how good someone becomes at desktop publishing, if he or she isn't a trained professional designer, certain skills will be lacking. A professional designer will also help to maintain consistency of your corporate image. You may also be fortunate enough to be in a library, university, or school district with an in-house professional designer. If so, it is a terrific option for the design of your publications. Talk with the designer to see if he or she can handle the additional work and what kind of production time it will take.

If you don't have an in-house designer or the budget to contract someone to do all of your design work, the best option is to have desktop publishing templates for your various publications designed when your corporate identity package is developed.

Then, you can use your desktop publishing skills to create different publications based on those templates. You will maintain your corporate identity and produce quality publications. If you use these templates, you may want to build in a fee for having the designer review publications produced with the templates on an annual basis. Your designer may even do this for free—it will be a chance to share tips for using the templates in the best graphic fashion.

In many cases, you will start with a lump sum available for your publication and then work backwards in terms of what you spend on each area. If you are working with an outside designer, you may want to tell the designer what you can spend and share your publication description with him or her. The designer can then either come back with a proposal for a publication that will meet your goal, staying within your budget, or tell you that what you are trying to do is unrealistic for the amount of money you have to spend. At that time, you can get a second opinion, alter parts of your plan, or go back to your library director, building principal, or library board for additional funding.

Printing

Once you have your design and know how many copies you want to print, you can approach printers for quotes. You can adjust your quantity, number of ink colors, or type of paper to stay within your budget. It is important to get a preliminary quote from a printer before you proceed with design on a project. You don't want to end up with a beautifully designed publication that you cannot afford to print.

Photos or Other Illustrations

If you plan to use photographs or to purchase illustrations for use in your publication, it is important to build this into your budget. Both can be quite expensive, and, if they are important to you, you must determine how much you can afford to spend on them. Get a quote from a photographer, an illustrator, or a stock photography or illustration company, and include that figure in your budget.

Distribution

If you plan to distribute this publication in your library, the distribution budget line item might actually be zero. If you plan to mail the publication by itself, however, or stuff it into someone else's mailing, you want to include those costs.

Bulk mailing is a viable option for most libraries because they can apply for nonprofit status. Schools, colleges, and universities may already have a bulk nonprofit permit that the library can use. Remember to include in your budget both the postage for mailing the item and the cost of preparing the mailing. You can either learn how to prepare bulk mail yourself or hire an outside mailing service to do it for you. Often, hiring an outside mailing service is the best option; such a service is very knowledgeable about postal regulations and can sort your mail so that you get the best possible postal rate. If you are going to prepare the mailing yourself, your local post office may offer a course or at least have a videotape that you can watch to learn how to prepare mailings. It will be important to refresh your knowledge on an annual basis as postal regulations are constantly changing.

If you will be mailing your publication nonprofit bulk rate or first class, take a mock-up of it to your post office or your mailing service and have it reviewed for mailing before you go to press. For instance, you may find out that, because your publication is an unusual size, it is going to be expensive to mail. Then you will have to decide between the uniqueness of your design or format and the impact that it will have on your distribution budget.

If you are including your publication as an insert in another mailing, such as the water department's bills, you may be asked to pay for part of the process of stuffing these inserts. At the time you agree to insert your materials, find out what costs you will be required to cover—it might still be a bargain compared to paying for separate preparation and postage.

Another option to consider for distributing your publication is having it stitched or inserted in another publication, such as the school district newsletter or the local newspaper. Investigate the costs of such distribution and think carefully about the kind of perception it will create. If you insert your public library's newsletter in the local newspaper will you be reaching your constituency or a much wider group? What will the costs be compared to mailing it separately to all of your cardholders?

Another wonderful distribution method is sending things home with children from schools. If you are a school librarian, this makes perfect sense. Public library materials may need to be approved by the superintendent of schools or school board before being distributed in this way, but, particularly for summer reading promotional materials, this method might make sense. Experience has shown, however, that there is a direct correlation between the age of the student and whether or not the item arrives at home. (The younger the students, the better chance of your publication making it to their home.)

DEVELOPING A PUBLICATION SCHEDULE

The best way to develop a publication schedule is backwards! Determine the date that you want the publication to be available and work backwards from that date. Determine how long it will take for your printer to do the printing. This gives you the date that you or your designer will need to send your artwork to the printer. Next decide how long it will take to design your publication. How long will it take to write the content? How long will you need between developing the copy plan and having the content written? Eventually, experience will provide you with time frames for these elements of your schedule. From the start, your designer and printer will be able to estimate time for their part of the process. A general guideline, however, is four weeks for each step in the process. A sample publication schedule appears in Figure 5.2.

This may not always be a realistic time schedule. Newsletters will probably need a tighter time schedule because you will want information to be timely when it reaches your readers. But always allow enough time for careful proofreading, editing, and checking of design and layout, and remember that a "rush" schedule may negatively impact your budget. Printers and designers often charge extra for "rush" projects, and rightly so.

NEWSLETTERS

Newsletters are an effective, if traditional, communications tool, particularly when you are trying to reach one specific target audience. Libraries of all types use monthly, bimonthly, and/or quarterly newsletters to promote their services, programs, and collections. Producing a newsletter on a regular basis can be a burden

---

FIGURE 5.2 Sample Publication Schedule

Publication Needed	May 1
To Printer	April 1
Copy to Designer	March 1
Copy Plan Developed	February 1

for library staff, however, and the content often suffers when the editors are overloaded with other work. It is important to consider whether or not a newsletter is the best tool for communicating your message.

DO YOU NEED ANOTHER NEWSLETTER?

A member of your library board may go to a conference and discover that lots of other public libraries have newsletters. He or she may return and deliver the decree that "Our library needs a newsletter." If that happens, the next questions should be "Why do we need a newsletter, what do we want to communicate, and to whom?"

Often, a new or stand-alone publication is not the best answer. There may be other ways of reaching your audience without incurring the additional expense and work a newsletter entails. For example, a public library might ask to have a monthly column or page in the city newsletter. This would save both production and distribution costs and also show the public that city agencies are cooperating. If there is no city newsletter, it might be worthwhile asking the parks department director if they have ever considered a newsletter. If the answer is "yes," consider a joint publication. If both the library and the parks department want to reach the parents of school-age children with a bimonthly publication, you can develop a slicker publication and circulate it more widely by pooling your resources. Such a plan has the additional benefit of presenting the positive image of two taxpayer-funded entities working together to save costs.

If you are a school library media specialist, it might be a good idea to request a regular column in the school district or neighborhood newsletter or newspaper. The answer is dependent on the audience that you have selected for your message. If you are trying to reach teachers and the school newsletter is geared to them, this is a good medium for your message. If you are trying to communicate with parents, a neighborhood newsletter or newspaper might be ideal. Often these publications are looking for reliable contributors who can produce good copy.

Any library considering developing its own newsletter should ask two questions: "Are there other publications that address the same audience that I am trying to reach? Might I be able to obtain regular space in the appropriate publication?" If the answers are "yes," consider the quality and reputation of the publication before you decide to go in this direction. For instance, if your school district has a newsletter that is considered an important source of information for the parents you are trying to reach, and if parents really do read it, that is definitely where you want to be. On the other hand, if you are a public librarian and your city mails a monthly newsletter to all taxpayers, but it is regularly riddled with errors and ridiculed in the community, publishing your own newsletter is probably a better idea.

You should also think about how much time your target audience has available to read another publication. Young parents might not need another piece of "junk mail" to deal with every month, but senior citizens might welcome an information-filled publication that arrives regularly from the public library. Your Friends of the Library members might use a monthly newsletter as another membership perk and provide you with some funding. Parents of the children who use your school library media center might appreciate learning about the homework resources available at your library and reading about the interesting projects their children are doing in your library. If you decide that a newsletter is the best communications tool for your audience, thinking about the amount of time that your audience has available for reading the publication will help you shape content (the subject, length, and style of your articles) and will help you design the publication.

One reason for your library to consider publishing a newsletter is to help create and enhance its public image as part of the development of your corporate identity. A high-quality newsletter with a distinctive design that is consistent with the library's corporate identity and that includes informative articles can help create the perception that your library is an important community institution that offers quality service.

DEVELOPING YOUR NEWSLETTER

Once you decide you are ready to develop a newsletter for your library, you will need to assess the resources available to you. How much time can someone spend on the writing, editing, and distribution of the newsletter? Who will do the layout and design? Will you hire an outside graphic designer or will you have to desktop publish the newsletter yourself? How much money does your library have to spend on the project? Is there a print shop in your library, school district, or university that can do the printing for free or at a reduced cost? Are there inexpensive ways, such as the campus mail, to distribute the publication?

Writing a publication description for your newsletter will help you determine the resources necessary for your publication. Then you can develop a budget based on what you want and determine what you can afford. Figure 5.3 outlines a newsletter publication description.

FIGURE 5.3 Publication Description Outline—Newsletter

Purpose: Describe the goal of your newsletter. What do you want to communicate or promote?

Description: This should be a physical description of the newsletter. What size are you thinking about? How many colors of ink would you like to use? How many pages will your newsletter be? Remember, standard formats (11-by-17-inch paper, folded for 4 pages; 8 1/2-by-11-inch, folded for 4 pages) will save you money.

Publication Dates: How often will your newsletter be published? If quarterly, indicate publication month.

Audience: Provide a detailed list of your audience with a ballpark number of members of each group (for example, parents of school-age children in our community—10,000; all members of the friends of the library—2,000).

Number Produced: Based on your audience, how many newsletters do you plan to print?

Cost: Use the information that you put in this description to determine how much your newsletter will cost. Then go back to your overall communications budget and see if you can afford what you are planning. If you cannot, you may need to adjust your description to reflect a newsletter that works within your budget.

Content: What kind of information do you want to include in your newsletter? What regular columns or standing "headlines" will you have? For example, every issue might include a calendar of events and an annotated list of new books.

Issue Descriptions (optional): If you plan to publish "theme" issues of your newsletter, list them and the specific issue here (for example, a back-to-school issue in September).

Distribution: How are you going to get your newsletter out to its intended audience? Information racks in your library? Bulk mail? Send it home with students? How timely will the information included in your newsletter be? Will you need a distribution method that will get it there quickly?

Person Responsible: Who will be responsible for each task involved in producing and distributing the newsletter?

The next step is to determine, based on your resources, how much work will be done in-house and what you can afford to hire outside professionals to do. Use the information provided in the publication budget section (page 51) to think carefully about developing your newsletter's budget.

NEWSLETTER SCHEDULE

The production schedule for a newsletter may be tighter than for your other print publications, particularly if the newsletter includes a calendar of events or other timely information. The total time frame from copywriting to distribution might only be six weeks. Think about whether and how often you can manage this tight production schedule. You may wish to publish a bimonthly or quarterly newsletter instead of a monthly one—with monthly publications you are constantly in the middle of a production schedule.

You should also think about newsletter stories that can be produced in advance and used when space is available in an upcoming newsletter. For example, stories about on-going library services and collections will be interesting to your readers but don't necessarily have to run in a specific issue. This gives you content for each issue that can be prepared in advance so that the time closer to the publication date can be used to write articles on timely topics (such as the kick-off of your summer reading program or a new service policy recently passed by the board).

Above all, with a newsletter it is important to stick to your publication schedule. People should know when to expect it and learn to depend on the information they get from it. If you always mail it during the first week of the month, be consistent. This isn't always easy when you have competing priorities, but it is critical to the success of your newsletter.

BROCHURES

It seems that every business, every service, and every organization has a brochure! Your library may need one, too, or your library may need several brochures. If you are thinking about developing a brochure for one or more of your library's services, think carefully about the goal of this brochure and which goals or objectives in your public relations/communications plan it supports. Should you produce a variety of brochures for your library's different services and collections, or would investing in one high-quality overall brochure be the best approach? What you decide will depend on how you plan to use the brochure. For example, if you need a printed piece to give to new library cardholders telling them what is available to them, you will probably want to develop one brochure that describes all of your services and collections. If the head of reference services plans to visit local businesses to promote your library's business collection and services, however, a brochure geared to that audience with information about the business collection and service is the route that you want to go. As with most of your communications planning, it is a judgment call. The key is to produce effective materials that address your audience, and not to produce materials that are unnecessary, don't have a target audience, or don't further your plan.

Once you determine that you need a brochure and what you need it for, you are ready to think about design, budget, production schedule, and distribution. But, before you develop a publication description for it, think carefully about the elements of an effective brochure.

ELEMENTS OF AN EFFECTIVE BROCHURE

Think about the brochures that you pick up when you are traveling, visiting a museum, or walking through a shopping mall. Consider the brochures that come as "junk mail" and that you actually pick up and read! What do these brochures have in common? You will probably find that it is the following elements:

- **Eye-catching colors or artwork**
  Colors or artwork make you notice the brochure. The colors don't have to be bright, but they should be attractive to the eye. The artwork should draw you into the brochure's copy and tell you something about the type of information you are going to find in the brochure.

- **Clearly written, enticing copy**
  The copy or text of the brochure should be written clearly such that the person you want to attract will understand it. Don't be clever with words if they will confuse your message. Be succinct. Tell readers exactly what they need to know. For example, if you are developing a brochure to encourage small business owners to use your library's reference collection, the copy should describe the scope and variety of your collection and perhaps list a few exemplary titles—it doesn't need to provide a comprehensive list of titles in your collection.

- **Information about how to act**
A brochure that describes your library and its services should also include information about how a person can use the services. The address for the library, open hours, and perhaps a brief description of your cardholder requirements are all possibilities for information about "how to act." You won't get the results you want if you simply describe a valuable service or program, but fail to tell people how to take advantage of it.

BROCHURE PUBLICATION DESCRIPTION

Once you determine that you have a program or service you would like to promote via brochure, you should develop a publication description. This gives you a formal way to consider what you want to achieve with the brochure and how you are going to achieve it. An outline for a brochure publication description follows in Figure 5.4.

Once you determine what your brochure will look like and how it will be distributed, you will want to develop a budget and schedule. Use the information provided in the publication planning section to do this. The longer you think the life of your brochure will be, the more money you may want to invest in it. You may want to make a relatively major investment in the design of your library's overall service brochure because it's the first printed piece a new cardholder gets from you. In contrast, you may want to invest less in the design of the special brochure for your genealogy collection, because it will be used for public presentations during the month of September and then take its place in your literature racks after that.

ANNUAL REPORTS

Annual reports have traditionally been the way that corporations tell their stockholders the past year's story. They highlight successes and challenges and share information about the financial status of the organization. In some states, public libraries are required by law to publish an annual report that includes certain financial information. Some have chosen simply to publish the financial data and make them available to the public on request; others have seen the public relations potential in publishing an annual report that tells the whole story—not just the financial

FIGURE 5.4 Publication Description Outline: Brochure

Purpose: What is the goal of this brochure? What do you want to communicate or promote? Think about how it relates to your library's overall communications goal. Are there other services or collections that should be included in this brochure?

Description: This should be a physical description of the brochure. What size are you thinking about? How many colors of ink would you like to use? Will it include photos? When determining the format for a brochure, think about how you want to distribute it. If you want to put it in pre-existing information racks at your library, make sure the format you choose will display nicely in those racks. If you want to mail it in an envelope, be sure it is the size of a standard envelope. If you want it to be a self-mailer, be sure that a mailing panel is included in the design.

Publication Dates: How often will this brochure be reviewed for updating?

Audience: Provide a detailed list of your audience with a ballpark number of members of each group.

Number Produced: Based on your audience, planned distribution, and revision schedule, how many copies of this item do you plan to print?

Cost: Use the information that you put in this description to determine how much your brochure will cost. Then go back to your overall communications budget and see if you can afford what you are planning. If you cannot, may need to adjust your description to reflect a brochure that works within your budget.

Content: What will the content of the brochure be? How will it address the audience?

Distribution: Will you place the brochure in information racks? Mail it to a specific audience? Will staff members use it when they make public presentations?

Person Responsible: Who is responsible for the production of this brochure? This person is responsible for seeing that the publication is reviewed for revision on schedule, that the planned distribution occurs, and that it stays on its publication schedule. This person must also maintain an inventory of the brochure after it is printed so that you don't run out.

story. Still other libraries that don't necessarily have a legal obligation to publish a report have realized their responsibility to provide information to the community, as well as the public relations that they can get from an annual report; they develop and disseminate a report on an annual basis.

The first thing to decide if you plan to publish an annual report is who the audience is for the report. If you will use it primarily with potential donors and sponsors, you will probably develop a different report from the one that you distribute to all of your library users. For example, you might publish a slick, corporate-looking annual report for your fundraising efforts and you might also publish some brief information (data on use and finances along with bulleted highlights of the last year) on plastic bookbags that you give to library users at checkout. As with any of your print publications, format should follow function as you determine what type of annual report to develop.

While publishing an elegant annual report can be a rewarding project and can represent your library in a positive light, be sure that your report is consistent with your message. For example, if your financial data and narrative will indicate that it has been a rough budget year for your library, don't publish an annual report that looks expensive. A simple but elegant, one-color publication on attractive paper is probably more appropriate than a slick four-color book with photographs.

ELEMENTS OF AN EFFECTIVE ANNUAL REPORT

No matter what format you choose for your annual report or who your targeted audience is, certain elements are important for any effective annual report.

- Message
  Your annual report should be developed around a clear message and that message should be the one that has guided your past year's public relations efforts. This may mean that not every library program or service is mentioned in each year's report, but it is the best way to ensure that your annual report supports the public relations message that you have worked so hard to disseminate.

- Design that supports your corporate identity
  While you may want your annual report to be special or a little different from the materials that your library publishes on a regular basis, it should be designed based on your corporate identity. It may have some enhancements or include some more elegant elements than your monthly newsletter,

but someone should be able to glance at your annual report and know that it is a library publication.

- Letter from the library director
  This letter should summarize the past year. It should include highlights and challenges and clearly focus on your overall public relations message. For example, if you have built your public relations plan around the message that "our library is a community center," then the library director's letter should emphasize that message.

- Narrative of the year-in-review
  The length of this narrative is dependent on the size and format of your report, but it is important to call attention to highlights from the past year. Be sure that you don't repeat information that the director called attention to in his message; this is a chance to focus on other events and activities. For example, if you had a particularly successful summer reading program or series of adult programs, you might want to highlight the actual events here and the library director's letter might call attention to circulation increases that resulted from those programs.

- Circulation and other use information
  This information helps the reader see how your library is being used. It should be presented in an easy-to-understand fashion, such as charts or graphs. You may want to think about different ways of presenting the information based on your library's overall message and the most accurate demonstration of what really happened during the past year. For example, you might want to publish circulation and gate-count information in bar graphs by branch library to show that the branch library you are planning to close next year has limited use in comparison to other libraries. Or you might want to publish your circulation by collection because it demonstrates the high use of your children's collection—and you are about to mount a fundraising campaign for children's books. This doesn't mean that you should skew the information, but you can publish it in a way that supports your library's message and goals.

- Financial information
  If you are in a library that is mandated by state law to publish financial information, you may have little flexibility here. If you are able to make your own decisions about what you

publish, however, you should think carefully about your audience. If your report is targeted at the general population, simple financial data focusing on broad general areas will get your message across and not confuse people. If you are trying to show the expenses incurred by each library branch, you might want to break the figures out by facility. An annual report published primarily as a fundraising tool should probably include a list of donors and their levels of contribution so that potential donors have that information readily available. The key is to provide just the amount of financial information that your target audience needs—no more, no less. You may want to "test" your annual report copy with a couple of members of your target audience, a supportive corporate sponsor, or your Friends of the Library president to see if you are taking the right approach.

- Photographs of library board members
  If you can afford it, including photographs of your library board members in the annual report is a wonderful way to recognize board members and to remind the public that community members are involved in the operation of the library. You may have to invest in portrait photographs but they should be usable for several years of annual reports as well as for other publications, such as your newsletter or the newspaper.

DISSEMINATION

When you determine the target audience for your annual report, think carefully about how you will disseminate it. Mailing an annual report may be more costly than mailing a newsletter, but there is no reason to spend money on an annual report that sits on the shelf in your office and doesn't reach its intended audience. The bookbag idea mentioned above is a great way to disseminate an annual report targeted at the public. Bookmarks might be another format that would facilitate dissemination. Even if you publish a traditional booklet annual report, you may want to put a few copies in your library's pamphlet rack for the public to pick up. If your annual report targets corporate sponsors, you may want to mail copies to the past year's contributors and then use the report throughout the next year to solicit other contributions.

Another audience for annual reports is the library community. Establishing a mailing list of other libraries in your state or region and mailing a copy of your report to their directors helps you to build a professional network. These libraries will probably include your library on the mailing list for their reports; this exchange will help you to share ideas and strategies and also will keep you abreast of what is happening in other libraries in your area.

SCHOOL AND ACADEMIC LIBRARIES

While school and academic libraries may not find it practical to publish their own annual reports, they should work with their organizations' communications offices to be sure that the library is mentioned in the annual report. At the time of the year when the annual report is being developed, a note to the communications director reminding him or her of the library's accomplishments during the past year (and perhaps an offer to help compile copy and photographs illustrating those accomplishments) might be just what an overworked communications director needs. Even if this strategy isn't successful the first time, over time it may prove fruitful and the library and its accomplishments will be a part of the organization's overall communications focus.

OTHER PRINTED MATERIALS

Of course, the printed materials that your library produces will not be limited to brochures, newsletters and annual reports. You will probably want to develop flyers, posters, bookmarks, booklists, and other types of printed promotional materials. The development process for each of these items should mirror the processes described for newsletters and brochures. The difference for such items as flyers and bookmarks is that they may be more ephemeral—less permanent items than a service brochure that you will use for several years or a newsletter that you publish on a regular basis.

Developing and using a design template for all of your library's program flyers and posters will save you time and help you maintain the corporate identity that you have established. You need only open that template on your computer, key in the copy for an upcoming program, and make the number of copies that you need. You may wish to develop several templates with a similar look but that will appeal to different age groups.

USING PHOTOGRAPHS

Photographs can be a wonderful addition to any publication. With high-quality reproduction techniques and the availability of quality scanners, photographs are much less expensive to use than they once were. Even color photos reproduce well in black and white. Including photographs, particularly of people, in newsletters adds to reader interest. It is exciting, for instance, for parents to see their children pictured at storytime in your monthly newsletter.

You may want to think carefully about using photographs of people or places in your brochures. If you plan to update the brochure only once every few years, the photos can quickly become dated. For example, you may produce a brochure for your library's new grants information center and put a photograph of the center's two staff members right smack in the middle of the brochure's cover. If they both resign in the next two months, your brochure is obsolete. On the other hand, a photo of adorable children at storytime in the brochure for your children's services department may never become dated—even when the adorable children are in junior high!

Before using any photographs of people in your publications, however, be sure you have the appropriate signed releases. You may want to check with your legal department or school district or university central office to determine what type of release is required by law.

TIPS FOR CREATING PRINT PUBLICATIONS

Creating effective print publications requires careful planning and close attention to detail. The process also provides an opportunity to get the creative juices flowing and produce materials that are eye-catching and interesting for your audience. The checklists that follow in Figures 5.5 and 5.6 will help you pay attention to detail while developing an interesting publication. They will remind you of each step in the process even when you are working on a rush job. Use them for each project that you develop. You may wish to add other items to each list to reflect your particular publication development process.

The Design Checklist in Figure 5.5 is the overall checklist for the development of your publication. It will remind you to check each element of design and copy for consistency and accuracy.

The Proofing Checklist in Figure 5.6 will help guide you through the process of proofreading your publications. Make three copies of the publication mock-up and attach a copy of the checklist to each one. Then, ask three colleagues to proofread it. You will be amazed at the errors they find that evaded your careful eyes. For some reason, when a person spends many hours working on a publication his or her eyes play tricks and miss errors when proofreading. Three other sets of eyes will help ensure accuracy of the information in your publication and avoid embarrassing typos. Of course, you should still proofread the publication yourself. There are certain things, such as the spelling of people's names, that only you, as the person responsible for the publication, may be in a position to check.

Completing the Printing Specifications form in Figure 5.7 will help you remember all the important details that you need to provide the printer. Fill out the form and then make a photocopy for your files. You can send this completed form to several printers when you are soliciting bids for your job. It will provide them with all of the pertinent information that they will need for quoting the job. Your copy of the form will also help you solve any problems that come up with the printing job, such as the printer using the wrong paper or folding the project the wrong way. It is your proof of the information that you provided to the printer.

DEVELOP, DESIGN, PRINT, AND DISSEMINATE

Developing, designing, and printing promotional publications is a highly creative process that can be a lot of fun because of the creativity that it involves. In addition, it can be a highly effective way to promote the programs, services, and resources of your library. Just remember as you are developing those publications and devoting your library's fiscal and human resources to them, that it is always important to have an effective means of disseminating the publications. The real value of printed promotional materials is only realized when they reach their intended audience. Then you will see the impact of your work as the target audience acts on the compelling promotional information that you have developed.

FIGURE 5.5 Design Checklist

Project Description _____

Person Responsible for the Project _____

_____Is the document page size correct for the final document?

_____Are all of the margins consistent?

_____Have you run a spell check on the document?

_____Are all of the headlines, subheads, and text styles consistent throughout the publication?

_____Is the spacing throughout the publication consistent?

_____Have you printed out and proofread the hard copy?

_____Have you asked at least two colleagues to proofread the hard copy?

_____Have you completed the proofing checklist?

_____Have you completed the printing specifications checklist?

_____

Signature   Date

Date project transmitted to printer _____

FIGURE 5.6 Proofing Checklist

Project Description _____

Person Responsible for the Project _____

Items to Check	Approved	Changes/Comments
Address numbers and locations		
Postal information (permits, symbols, return addresses, placement, barcodes)		
Names, titles, and affiliations (printing and accuracy)		
Copy in general (word omissions, grammar)		
Photos		
Captions (Is the right caption under the right photo or art? Is the right name under the right person?)		
Page numbers (Is the sequence correct?)		
Sizes (Check all dimensions.)		
FINAL PROOFING Have all the revisions noted above been made?		

_____

Signature   Date

FIGURE 5.7 Printing Specifications

Person Responsible for the Project _____

Phone Number _____

Date Project is Needed

Details

Size

Folding (if any)

Number of pages

Number of colors

Art

Number of photos

Number of illustrations

Paper Specifications

Type and Weight

Quantity

Delivery Information

_____

_____

_____

Printer Used:

Name _____

Address _____

Phone _____

Working with Printers: An Interview

Mark Moroney, of N&M Design, Elmhurst, Illinois, has been involved in the printing industry for more than 20 years. I talked with him regarding effective library relationships with printers. Moroney says that working with a printer is all about "relationship." He says, "You want someone who is there when you need them, who you can talk to and who you can trust." Building this relationship may take time and some trial and error. It is probably a good idea to try working with a number of printers and/or brokers who sell printing for a variety of print shops and learn where you get the best service and develop the strongest relationship. Moroney says this relationship is harder to build when you do a small volume of printing. "It isn't the size of the jobs that matters. It is the number of jobs." A printer who knows you will be returning to him with several jobs throughout the year will work harder to develop a relationship with you. However, Moroney admits, "You will probably pay a little more for fairness and consistency from your printer." Working with a printer who will be honest and fair with you is particularly important if you don't know a lot about the technical aspects of printing.

One important thing for someone who is just learning about the printing industry to understand is spoilage. When you ask for a quote, the printer will base his number on 5–10% more paper than the quantity that you actually need. He will determine the percentage based on the difficulty of the print job. Heavy ink coverage, ghosting, and other special design techniques are among the things he will take into consideration. The additional percentage of paper is necessary to produce the final quantity that you need. And the percentage of increase gets smaller as the job gets larger. For example, on a printing job where you need only 500 pieces, the printer may base his quote on as much as 1,000; a 10,000 piece job, 12,000; and a 20,000 piece job, 22,000. This is because spoilage typically occurs in the first two to three hundred sheets of paper that run through the printing press.

Finally, Moroney warns that you should know what you are buying. If you have a low budget project, don't go to a high end printer. You may want your summer reading materials to look great, but only for the summer. Don't let a printer talk you into expensive varnishes to protect the ink on a project like that. Now, your annual report is another story. This is a special piece and you may want to go to a higher end printer and spend more money. This piece is going to represent a particular year in your library's history. Consider what you are printing before you decide who will do the printing. There are different levels of printers in terms of quality and while you want professional looking materials, you probably don't need to go to the most expensive printer in town.

6 MEDIA COVERAGE

Media coverage—an article in your local newspaper, a story on the 6 o'clock news—can be the most inexpensive and effective (and, at times, destructive) communications resource available. The coverage is free and it reaches a wide audience. Positive coverage from the media can help you achieve your public relations goal; if your story isn't presented in a positive light, it can set back both your public relations efforts and progress towards your library's goals. It is just as important to plan in advance how to handle unanticipated media coverage as it is to seek media coverage. Building effective relationships with reporters, editors, and photographers allows you to help each other achieve your goals—they get their stories and you get to tell your story!

WHEN THE MEDIA CALLS

It is important to have an overall philosophy and a policy about how you will handle inquiries from reporters. If you are in a school, a university library, or a public library that is governed by a city or county policy, your challenge may not be to develop a philosophy and policy, but to determine how to interpret the parent or governing body's policy. Many large organizations insist that all inquiries be directed to an office of communications or public relations before they are referred to the appropriate individual. If that is the case in your organization, do not view that as a detriment to coverage. The referral process can buy you much-needed time to gather information, and can protect you when you don't want to comment on a negative story. On the other hand, you hope that your communications office will refer the reporter appropriately to talk to an expert on, for example, the role of school library media programs in education. You may wish to spend some time educating your school district's or university's communications director so that he or she understands the library issues and knows where to make referrals.

If you are in a smaller organization that doesn't have an overall media relations policy, develop one. Often the library director or assistant director is the first contact and then on down the chain of command. Once the interview is cleared with the appropriate spokesperson, the reporter might be referred to someone who knows more about the topic. For example, if it is a story about summer reading, it is most appropriate for the reporter to talk with the children's librarian. But, if the reporter is calling with specific questions about the library budget, it is important that the interview be cleared and possibly held with, the library director or public relations person. A media relations policy prevents a reporter from putting your circulation clerk on the spot with a question about a recently challenged book—the staff person can simply tell the reporter that the interview must be cleared by the library director. Such a policy protects the staff and helps ensure that the message you are communicating is clear, consistent, and, above all, accurate.

RESPONDING TO MEDIA INQUIRIES

Any inquiry from the media should be viewed as an opportunity for your library. Whether the reporter is calling because of an interesting news release that you sent him or because a patron has complained to the reporter about a book in your library's collection, any inquiry is an opportunity to share your library's story and to continue to educate the community about the library's services, resources, and philosophy. Many celebrities who receive coverage in the scandal sheets sold in grocery stores take the attitude that "any press is good press." This may not always be true, but any media inquiry is an opportunity for positive news coverage.

It is always best to respond to a reporter's inquiry—even if you have to tell the reporter that the needed information isn't currently available. You are beginning to build a relationship that will benefit you down the road when you want coverage. Remember also that libraries have a variety of resources that can help people in the news business. For example, when a reporter calls looking for a local high school's 1966 yearbook photograph of someone in the news, your prompt response may begin to build an impression in the reporter's mind that the library has many useful resources—you may have made a friend for the future when you want a story covered.

Here is another example of the opportunity present in any inquiry. A reporter calls your public library and asks for information about a patron in your database. You know that the library's policy on confidentiality of patron records prohibits you from sharing that information without a court order. Rather than simply telling the reporter, "No," and acting irritated, you can use this as a chance to explain the policy and the philosophy behind it, and maybe even fax the reporter a copy. The reporter may not use the information in this story, but you will have educated the reporter about how your library operates and why.

Be careful to share all information with reporters that the public has a right to have access to. For example, the budget for a public, school, or publicly funded college or university is typically public information. If you get a request from a reporter for a document and you are unsure about whether or not it should be shared, check with legal counsel for your library, school district or college or university before sending the reporter away empty-handed. If you can't get an answer right away, tell the reporter you will get back to him. The last thing a library wants is to be accused by the media of withholding public information. Such an accusation will come back to haunt you when you deal with an intellectual freedom issue in the future.

At library board meetings, always be sure that there are extra copies of board materials for the media. Preparing several board packets and having them available on a table in the back of the room is a good idea. Or you might wish to use handing them out as an opportunity to greet each reporter and offer your help in answering any questions that they may have. Be sure that reporters get complete board packets—it is confusing if board members refer to materials that the media don't have, and it may appear that you are trying to hide something.

The Value of "I Don't Know"

Be forthcoming, honest, and helpful, and make "I don't know, but I'll find out and call you" an important part of your vocabulary—even when you are interviewed for radio or television. It is preferable that reporters wait for the correct information than that they receive incomplete or erroneous information. Wrong information will diminish your credibility as a source and eventually reporters will stop contacting you or devalue the information that you provide to them. No one can fault you for saying, "I don't know." And the return phone call to the reporter with the information that you find is another chance to tell your library's story.

There's No Such Thing as "Off the Record"

Going "off the record" is dangerous stuff. In novels, in the movies, and on television, sources frequently go off the record with reporters. They share information that they don't want attributed to them or that they don't want included in the story. Sometimes this is done because the interviewee believes that the background is essential to understanding other issues, but, for legal or personal reasons, he or she doesn't want the information published or attributed. The idea is that the reporter is then bound by some moral code to honor the agreement that the information is off the record. The reality is that, particularly for individuals who are novices in working with the media, there is no such thing as "off the record." If you don't want to be quoted or you don't want the information included in a story, don't say it to a reporter. It puts you both in a bad position—you may offer some information that the reporter simply cannot avoid reporting, and you may risk your job for sharing the information. Again, be forthright, honest, and helpful, but don't share "off the record" confidential information with a reporter.

DEVELOPING A RELATIONSHIP WITH THE MEDIA

In many ways, the professions of journalism and librarianship share similar values, particularly in the areas of intellectual freedom and freedom of information. Libraries also have a variety of resources that can support reporters in their work. Use these resources to develop a strong relationship with members of the media. When a reporter drops by to do a story on preschool storytime, but mentions a business story he is working on, tell him about the new resources in your business section. Take every opportunity to tell reporters about areas other than the one you are discussing. If a reporter is doing a story on the lack of parking near your library, give her the information she wants and then tell her about the new bookmobile service that you have started so that elderly people don't have to struggle with the lack of parking. Turn every topic into a win-win situation for your library and the reporter!

When a reporter calls, return the call promptly. If you have been dissatisfied with the quality or quantity of news coverage that you have received in the past, and if encouraging more accurate coverage is a priority for your library, returning reporters' calls in a timely fashion could be a key to changing the coverage you have been receiving. The next time a library story comes up, the reporters may remember you were helpful.

When you have a photo opportunity at your library, call the newspaper photo editor or a photographer that you have worked with in the past. It may just be the day they need some stand-alone art for the front page. On the other hand, you may spend hours compiling information for a reporter on what you think is a terrific story, setting up interviews and so forth; that may be turn out to be the day that the mayor resigns or there is a terrible traffic accident. Don't give up! Be friendly, but be persistent. The reporter will remember the work you did and your investment will pay off down the road!

Listen carefully anytime you talk with a reporter. For example, you may be walking together after a library board meeting and the reporter may tell you that he is a Civil War history enthusiast. Jot that information in your Rolodex or in a notebook or file. Then when your library buys new books on the Civil War, you can send him a note calling his attention to the new resources. This gives you an excuse to contact him, and remind him that your library is there. It will be a positive experience for both of you—people are always flattered when others take note of their interests, and your follow-up will provide him with a positive feeling about both you and your library.

Many computer software packages are designed to help salespeople manage their contact information. An inexpensive "contacts" program might be a good tool for you to use to manage your media contacts. These database programs usually provide space for personal information, the best time to call, and a record of previous contacts.

Some of the things mentioned above may seem time-consuming. However, if you work slowly over time to build relationships with reporters in your community, there will be a time when it pays off. If media representatives like and trust you, you will have more straightforward and pleasant dealings in the future. Ultimately, building strong relationships with reporters, without compromising their integrity or yours, will result in positive, honest news coverage for your library. The story may not always be the one that you want told, but you will have the opportunity to share your side of things.

TOOLS FOR ENCOURAGING MEDIA COVERAGE

There are a variety of tools that you might wish to use to encourage media coverage of your library's story. They include news releases, news conferences, press kits, broadcast fax, e-mail, and letters to the editor. Some tools are simple and inexpensive and others can be quite costly.

It is important to consider what tool you will use based on the type of coverage that you want, the time frame for the coverage, and how complicated the story might be. Libraries of all types should also consider expense. It is important to have accurate, attractive, and, at times, clever materials to sell a story that you want covered, but you must always take into consideration the fact that the public is paying the bill. For example, using a press kit complete with confetti and party horns to announce the opening of a new branch library might initially seem like a great idea, but if this is the first new library opened in your city in 45 years, do you really need to spend so much money to encourage the coverage? What if a reporter decides to do a story on how much money you spent on those press kits and how many more books you could have bought instead for the new branch?

With the press, you constantly walk the fine line between developing effective, interesting materials and developing materials that might become targets of criticism. A good rule of thumb with the media is to focus on providing accurate, concise information and to save the clever gimmicks for other projects.

NEWS RELEASES

News releases are a way to communicate information as simple as an upcoming holiday closure to information as complicated as the conversion to your new circulation system. You can use a news release to announce a new program or service, a special event or a new policy.

A news release should be short and to the point—one page is best. It should be written in an inverted pyramid format, with the most important information first and the least important last. The information in a news release should answer the standard news questions: who? what? when? where? and why? Sometimes it is helpful to simple draft the answers to these questions before you begin writing your release—then you have an easy way to check that everything is included. As newspaperman Joseph Pulitzer used to say about news, the three most important things are "Accuracy, Accuracy, Accuracy."

The news release can be written on plain paper or on library letterhead; it should always include the name, address, phone number, (and e-mail address, if available) of your library with the name of a contact person. Also, it is important to include a release date so it is clear when the information can be published or announced. A news release should be double-spaced, printed on only one side of the paper. If it continues beyond one page, type MORE at the bottom of the page. Multiple pages should be stapled together in the upper left corner. Type ### or -30- at the end of your release (to indicate to the editor or reporter the end of the news item or article). If you are in a small community or if your community has weekly or neighborhood newspapers, you may be lucky enough to have your news releases published verbatim. Reporters at small weekly or daily papers are often grateful for well-written news releases that can be used as filler in their newspapers. Pay attention to the publications that print your information—you may want to develop longer, more detailed releases for those publications. This is an excellent opportunity for coverage.

Several sample news releases follow in Figures 6.1–6.3.

While you want to remind the press regularly that your library exists, you don't want them to think that you are personally trying to deforest the country by sending out as many news releases as possible. For example, if you want to promote the new preschool storytime schedule at your six branch libraries, try to get all of the information in one release. Don't send the major media separate releases for each branch. If you are targeting neighborhood newspapers, however, you might want to customize a special release for each newspaper, focusing on the schedule at their neighborhood's branch.

Typically, it is best to mail news releases to your local media at least two weeks prior to the event or program that you are announcing. Some publications may have calendars or columns that require more lead time. Contact them and find out. Sometimes you will have breaking news that needs a rush news release (such as the appointment of a new library director) and you may want to hand deliver or fax that release to an editor. But, don't make that a regular practice; do it only when you have something that you particularly want to receive special attention.

Don't follow up every news release with a phone call. Nothing is more annoying to a reporter or editor on deadline than a phone call from a public relations person wanting to know if a piece of paper, that wasn't solicited in the first place, was received in the mail. Choose carefully the releases that you follow up. Perhaps you did a release on a new service to the elderly and sent it to a reporter who, months before, had expressed an interest in that area. You may want to follow up with that particular reporter to see if you can provide any additional information on the topic. On the other hand, calling every reporter that you sent a news release announcing your Memorial Day closure is a waste of your time, will probably create ill will, and in the end could adversely affect the library's coverage.

Finally, if you have several releases to distribute at one time, by all means mail them in one envelope. You are saving an editor,

---

FIGURE 6.1 Sample News Release

FOR IMMEDIATE RELEASE

Contact: Jim Smith

(212) 999-9999

Reference Librarian

Smithville Public Library

NEW LIBRARY DIRECTOR HIRED

The Smithville Public Library Board of Trustees announced today that Jane Weaver has been hired as the new library director. Weaver will assume her post on March 7.

"We are excited that Ms. Weaver has agreed to lead the Smithville Public Library, " said Linda Workman, when announcing the appointment. "Her strong background in fundraising and building planning is exactly what our library needs at this time."

Weaver is currently the director of Johnsonville Public Library, a post she has held for six years. She has more than 15 years of public library experience as a library director, reference librarian, and children's librarian.

"I am excited about this new challenge," said Weaver. "It will be wonderful to work with the dedicated staff and board of the Smithville Public Library."

Weaver replaces Brenda Bixler who retired last year after 10 years as the director of Smithville Public Library.

-30-

FIGURE 6.2 Sample News Release

FOR IMMEDIATE RELEASE

Contact: Sue Johnson

(718) 555-5555

School Library-Media Specialist

Johnsonville Elementary School

STUDENTS DEMONSTRATE SURFING SKILLS

Third graders at Johnsonville Elementary School, 8503 W. Fisher St., will demonstrate their Internet surfing skills at an open house in the school library media center on Thursday, September 12, from 7:30 to 8 p.m.

Adults and other students will have the opportunity to explore the Internet and to see the Web Pages that the third graders have created.

At 8 p.m. there will be a special demonstration of CU-CMe technology as the students chat live with their keypals from the United Kingdom. This technology, which was donated for the evening by Ohio Internet Services, will allow the students to see each other for their first time. They have been communicating over the Internet for six months.

Virtual reality, live chat, and other technology will also be demonstrated during the event. Refreshments, donated by the Johnsonville Elementary School Parent Teacher Organization, will be served.

The open house is free and open the public. For more information, contact Susan Johnson at (718) 555–5555.

-30-

FIGURE 6.3 Sample News Release

FOR IMMEDIATE RELEASE

Contact: Marge Moore
           (302) 666-6666
           Library Director
           Moorefield College Library

COLLEGE LIBRARY INVITES PUBLIC USE

The doors of Moorefield College Library are open to the community, Joseph Kavanaugh, college president, recently announced.

"We want the community to be able to take advantage of the wonderful resources and services of our university's library," said Kavanaugh. "In addition, to offering the community free use of the library, we are also extending our night and weekend hours so that we will be open at more convenient times."

Library director Marge Moore said, "All community members have to do is stop by and apply for a library card. One piece of identification is all they need for access to our vast collections."

The library is now open from 8 a.m. to midnight, seven days each week. Moorefield College student body president Sharon Prince said, "This is great! The library is open more hours for us and the public will get to use it, too." She added, "I hope this will create better relations between members of the neighborhood and college students."

Founded in 1878, Moorefield College is a private, liberal arts college. More than 2,000 students attend classes on its three-acre downtown campus located at 484 Midview Avenue.

-30-

a reporter, or an intern the time of opening several envelopes from you—and you are saving your library money.

NEWS CONFERENCES

Before planning a news conference, decide if what you want to announce is really breaking news. Don't let the Junior League talk you into holding a news conference to announce their recent book donation if you don't think your local media is going to be interested in covering it. If you think that, for political reasons, you need to hold a news conference that the media might not be interested in, turn it into a special event. Invite staff and library supporters, have a speaker, and serve refreshments. That way, when the press doesn't show, the Junior League members present won't be disappointed. You are still celebrating their donation!

If you do have something of high news value to announce, such as the appointment of a new library director, a news conference may be the best tool for making the announcement. Choose a time and location convenient for the members of the press to attend. For example, don't schedule a news conference one hour before deadline at the daily paper and expect an article to appear that day, or at 5 p.m. and expect the story to be on the 6 o'clock news. Be sure there is parking available for the press at the location you choose and plenty of outlets in the room for the videographers to plug in their lights.

Announce your news conference as far in advance as possible. You can mail or fax a news release or, depending on the time frame, make personal phone calls. Include all pertinent information in your release, but save some "news" for the news conference. For example, tell them that you are going to announce the appointment of the new library director, but save the "who" for the news conference.

Rehearse your news conference. Have each participant show up an hour early and walk through the way that you will conduct the conference. Ask participants a few of the questions you anticipate being asked at the news conference so that they can begin to think through their answers.

After the news conference, different media outlets may want varied angles on the story. Think about this before the news conference. Identify staff to work with reporters from different stations and newspapers. Take camera crews to different areas in the library so that each media outlet gets a unique angle on the same story.

One final note on the news conference—use it sparingly! Li-

Tips for a Successful News Conference
• Start on time. If you have planned your news conference for 10 a.m., start at 10 a.m., particularly if any media representatives are there. Don't wait for Channel 5 to arrive if Channel 2 and 10 are already there. • Develop a script and follow it. Make sure that everyone involved in the news conference has a copy of the script and understands his or her role. A quick walk-through prior to the event will help to ensure this. Don't deviate. If you announce at the beginning that questions will be addressed at the end, do that even if reporters try to ask questions while you are making your prepared presentation. It is your news conference and you want to maintain control of it. • Keep it short. The prepared part of your news conference should never take more than 15 to 20 minutes, and the entire event with questions should not exceed an hour. Again, this will help you maintain control, particularly if you are dealing with a controversial issue.

braries aren't police departments. They shouldn't have many stories that demand news conferences. If you do have something "hot" to announce, such as the outcome of a censorship challenge, schedule a news conference. For other news and information, use such tools as news releases, public service announcements, and newsletters. Don't demand that the press show up at a specific time and place if the "news" doesn't warrant it. Use other times when the media might already be in attendance (for example, library board meetings, city council meetings, and special events) for such activities as accepting donations from generous community groups.

PRESS KITS

When you have a particularly special event or series of events to promote, or when you need to communicate a lot of information about a complex issue, you may want to develop a press kit. A press kit is usually a packet of materials promoting an event or service or providing information about an issue.

Items to Include in a Press Kit

A press kit is usually focused on a particular issue or event, but you will want to think about including a variety of materials in it. For example:

- A list of materials in the kit. This list will help the reporter identify each item in the kit. Provide a brief (one to two sentence) description of each item.
- A news release describing the particular issue or event. This should be prominent in the kit no matter what format you choose.
- A fact sheet about the issue or event and/or a fact sheet about your library. This provides bulleted information that is easy to access. It probably will repeat some of what is in the news release, but it provides a reporter with a quick overview.
- Support materials. If you are promoting summer reading, include your summer reading materials. If you are trying to draw attention to your bond issue, put in your campaign materials. Information in a press kit should go beyond what a reporter gets in a news release.
- Relevant photographs. If the press kit is for the groundbreaking of your new library and you have a photograph of an artist's rendering of the new building, make copies and put it in the press kit. If you are announcing your new library director, include that person's picture. Don't include photos if they don't enhance the story.
- A list of contacts. Give reporters a list of people that they can talk to about the story. If you are announcing the new corporate sponsorship of your children's programming, you could include the children's librarian, the library director, and representatives of the new corporate sponsor. Be sure that everyone included on the list has been briefed on the story and knows that he or she will be listed as a contact.
- Annual report. Based on the story, you may want to include a copy of your library's most recent annual report. Think about whether or not it is relevant. A copy of last year's annual report might provide information to support the announcement of a new bond issue or fundraising campaign; it might not be relevant to the announcement of a new series of adult programs.
- Your business card. If you are the library's primary press contact, be sure that your business card and contact information are included in the press kit.

Press Kit Formats

Some organizations use formats other than packets in the hopes that their materials will stand out in a reporter's pile of mail. The warning earlier in this chapter about spending too much money developing clever formats for press kits is worth repeating. If you do decide, however, to develop a special format for your press kit, consider asking your Friends of the Library, or the Parent Teachers Organization to fund the project. Be sure to give them full credit on the materials ("This packet printed courtesy of . . .) to avoid any accusations of "frittering away taxpayer dollars." Whatever format you choose for your press kit, don't get so caught up in being clever and creative that you accidentally end up distributing information that isn't accurate, clear, and easy to use.

Disseminating Press Kits

A press kit might be a good way to promote your library's annual summer reading program. It could include a news release describing the program, a calendar of events, the summer reading promotional materials, and a list of photo opportunities throughout the summer. Because a press kit is more costly to produce than an individual news release, you probably don't want to mail one to everyone on your media list. Including a note on the bottom of a general news release—"press kit available on request"—is a good approach. Then, target particular reporters and hand deliver the kits at a convenient time or mail them with a personalized letter. If you invest time and money in developing these kits, you want to make sure you get the most possible mileage out of them.

You might also decide to develop a press kit that includes comprehensive information about your public library's services and resources to distribute during National Library Week. After this annual celebration, the press kit is a useful resource to give to reporters upon request or to send to a new reporter assigned to cover the library.

Like news conferences, press kits should be used sparingly. They are an effective tool when you have an event, an issue, or a service that you want to receive particular attention, and they can be used to provide the media with comprehensive information about your library and its programs.

BROADCAST FAX

Broadcast faxing is becoming a more and more popular way for public relations practitioners to spread the word. However, the reaction from the media is mixed. "Junk fax" is harder to deal with than junk mail. When unsolicited mail arrives, a reporter can put it aside until he has time to deal with it. When an unsolicited fax is received, it ties up the newsroom's fax machine whether or not anyone wants it. In general, you should save the fax for times when a reporter requests specific information that you need send quickly, or when you truly have breaking news to report (for example, your library will be closed for two days because of broken pipes).

E-MAIL

If the members of the press in your community have e-mail addresses, e-mail is a good alternative to faxing and "snail-mailing" news releases. Since e-mail is becoming prevalent throughout the country, you may want to consider sending your news releases to reporters this way—or you might at least use e-mail for follow up. Reporters' e-mail boxes will probably soon begin to fill up with junk mail, but, like "snail mail," e-mail is unobtrusive; unlike a phone call, it doesn't demand immediate attention; unlike a fax, it doesn't tie up a phone line; and it is faster than all the alternatives.

Ask the reporters you work with if they have e-mail and if they would like you to use it to communicate with them. If the answer is "yes," by all means use it! You will save many trees by printing fewer news releases—and e-mail provides the opportunity for "conversation" between you and the reporter. If the reporter is interested in the story in your release, has questions, or needs more information, all the reporter has to do is "reply."

LETTERS TO THE EDITOR

If you receive news coverage and the facts are blatantly wrong, if you have a story that you can't seem to get covered, or if you must receive mention in the newspaper, you can write a letter to the editor. For instance, if you have trouble getting the newspaper to announce the Junior League's recent donation, a thank-you letter to the editor might be a solution. Or if the paper publishes an article stating that your library director's salary is $20,000 more than it really is and then refuses to run a correction, the letter to the editor might be the way to get the correct information published. This is another tool you should use sparingly, however, to avoid being perceived as a "whiner." Also, if you only submit a letter on an occasional basis, you have a better chance of the newspaper publishing it.

The first thing to decide is who the letter should be from. Perhaps it is better that the letter be signed by your library board chair, principal, or library director. Draft it under that person's name and then be sure to get approval before submitting it to the newspaper.

Most newspapers publish specific guidelines for letters to the editor. Follow them carefully. Again, your letter has a better chance of being published if it doesn't require a lot of editing or a follow-up phone call for more information.

SPECIAL TOOLS TO ENCOURAGE TELEVISION AND RADIO COVERAGE

In most cases, the tools described above will work to encourage both print and broadcast coverage of your library. But there are some other tools, such as public service announcements and video news releases, that can be used specifically to target broadcast media attention.

PUBLIC SERVICE ANNOUNCEMENTS

Public service announcements (PSAs) are written statements to be read on the radio or on television. You may wish to develop public service announcements for your local radio or television stations to use to spread your library's message. Before you put time and energy into developing them, contact your target media outlet and find out what they are most likely to use. In many instances, radio and television reporters prefer to take your regular news release and adapt it for their use. In some cases, they may want it written as a public service announcement, and, in still other instances, they may be interested in broadcasting a prerecorded or videotaped version of your announcement.

Public service announcements should be typed in all capital letters and triple spaced. You should write several versions that take different amounts of time to read. A good guide for estimating the time for a public service announcement is 2.5 words per second. Figures 6.4–6.6 are examples of public service announcements of varying lengths.

If you have a special message to relay and if your local radio stations will air prerecorded PSAs, you might want local celebrities, such as the mayor or a professional athlete who is a hometown boy, to record your PSAs. Special celebrations like National Library Week or Children's Book Week are times when you might want to produce PSAs that talk about the role that libraries play in your community. If you keep the message in your prerecorded PSA generic, it can be used over a longer period of time. You probably won't want to produce prerecorded PSAs to promote a one-shot special event or program at your library.

FIGURE 6.4 Sample Public Service Announcement

PUBLIC SERVICE ANNOUNCEMENT
MOOREFIELD COLLEGE LIBRARY

FOR IMMEDIATE RELEASE

Contact: Marge Moore
            Library Director
            (212) 888-8888

                                                    10 SECONDS

                                            KILL: November 1, 1997

THE DOORS OF THE MOOREFIELD COLLEGE LIBRARY ARE OPEN TO
EVERYONE...

DAILY FROM EIGHT A.M. TO MIDNIGHT....

COME VISIT US AT FOUR-EIGHT-FOUR MIDVIEW AVENUE.

FIGURE 6.5 Sample Public Service Announcement

PUBLIC SERVICE ANNOUNCEMENT
SMITHVILLE PUBLIC LIBRARY

FOR IMMEDIATE RELEASE

Contact: Jim Smith
Reference Librarian
(608) 999-9999

20 SECONDS
KILL: December 1, 1997

YOU CAN VISIT THE SMITHVILLE PUBLIC LIBRARY AND NEVER LEAVE HOME....

DIAL THE LIBRARY FREE ON YOUR COMPUTER AT FIVE-FIVE-FIVE-ONE-TWO-THREE-EIGHT...

BROWSE THE SHELVES, REQUEST A BOOK, OR ACCESS THE MANY ELECTRONIC DATABASES...

DIAL THE LIBRARY TODAY.

FIGURE 6.6 Sample Public Service Announcement

PUBLIC SERVICE ANNOUNCEMENT
WELLTOWN PUBLIC LIBRARY

FOR IMMEDIATE RELEASE

Contact: Bill Wells
               Public Information Officer
               (212) 666-6666

                                                30 SECONDS
                                                KILL: July 1, 1997

ADULTS, CHILDREN, AND TEENS...

GRAB YOUR MAGNIFYING GLASSES AND RUN TO WELLSVILLE PUBLIC
LIBRARY...

HELP SOLVE A MYSTERY BY PARTICIPATING IN THE FREE MYSTERIOUS
SUMMER READING PROGRAM...

ATTEND PROGRAMS, READ GREAT BOOKS, AND WIN GREAT PRIZES...

ANYONE CAN READ TEN BOOKS AND EARN A TICKET TO MAGICIAN DAVID
COPPERFIELD'S AUGUST TWELFTH WELLSVILLE PERFORMANCE...

CALL THE LIBRARY TODAY AT THREE-NINE-SEVEN-EIGHT-ONE-FOUR-NINE FOR
MORE INFORMATION.

Video public service announcements for television are expensive to produce; before developing them be sure that the local television stations are willing to air them. A television station in your community might be more interested in producing a public service announcement for you using some of its on-air news talent. Having the anchor from the 6 o'clock news appear in a public service announcement for the local public library is a win-win opportunity for both your library and the television station—the television station gets a unique public service announcement that says something positive about their on-air talent and your library gets its message out. Radio stations may also be interested in producing prerecorded public service announcements using their on-air celebrities.

VIDEO NEWS RELEASES

A video news release (VNR) is exactly what you would expect—a video version of a news release. Some VNRs are so sophisticated in their production quality that they look as if they were produced by a television news team. They are expensive to produce and rarely aired. Before considering producing a video news release, check with your local television stations and find out whether they would use them.

You might seriously consider producing a VNR when you have something visual that you really want the media to see because it sells your story. For example, if you are putting a bond issue for new library buildings on the ballot and you want the media to see your main library building's crumbling foundation, a VNR may be the best way to get their attention. But think carefully before you invest the time and money required to produce a quality VNR.

GETTING YOUR STORY COVERED

While it may often seem that getting your library's story covered by the local media is a matter of luck, strategically targeting various media outlets, being aware of the story possibilities at your library, and building relationships with reporters, producers, and editors will help increase your chances for coverage. Most importantly, don't give up. If you spend three days providing a reporter with background and interviews for a story and then there is a national or local crisis, you have every right to be disappointed if your story is dropped, but your efforts have not been in vain. If you carefully select the media outlet for your story and then develop your message especially for the selected outlet, however, you have a better chance of success.

CHOOSING YOUR MEDIA OUTLET

At times you will have a special story that you want to "sell" to a newspaper or radio or television station for coverage. Before you start setting up appointments and mailing information to reporters, check out the demographics of the media outlet and make sure that their audience is the one you want to reach. If you want to tell senior citizens about the afternoon concerts you are hosting at your library, approaching the local rock radio station may not be the best strategy. Any media outlet that accepts advertising will have demographic descriptions available of its audience. Call and ask. There may also be a publication in your community compiling that information for all local media. Do a little research about the media in your community and develop a file for each outlet that might provide coverage for your library. Develop a fact sheet for each media outlet. Sample fact sheets for print and broadcast media appear in Figures 6.7–6.9.

Approaching the right outlet for your story will not only help you reach your target audience; you will also have a better chance of success in getting coverage. The reporter or news editor will see that the story is appropriate for his or her audience.

If you are trying to sell a story, be smart about when you call. Find out when deadline is and never call within the hours before or after deadline. Include information about deadlines on your fact sheet. Ask a reporter when is the best time to call. Have a script or notes for your call. Be ready to deliver materials to the station or newspaper after the call or to fax them or send them by messenger.

One final note: Targeting stories doesn't mean that you turn down opportunities for coverage. If the rock-and-roll radio station wants to do a story on library services for the elderly, go for it! Maybe they know something that isn't reflected in their demographics. Basically, if you want to encourage news coverage of your library and its services, assist with every inquiry!

STORIES IN THE DRAWER

Libraries have many stories. However, many library-related stories are not time-sensitive. The fact that your school library media center has a parenting collection and that parents visit after school and share books with their children might make a won-

FIGURE 6.7 Sample Media Fact Sheet: Newspaper or Magazine

Name of Publication:

Format: What kind of news does this paper cover (e.g., local, national, international)?

Publication Schedule: Is it a daily, weekly, or monthly publication? If it is daily, what time of day is it published?

Circulation: How many copies of this publication are circulated?

News Release Requirements: Call and ask! Most newspapers will be very specific.

Staff/Work Hours/Topics Covered/Best Time to Contact: List your contacts here. Find out the best time to call them and what "beats" they each cover.

Mailing Address:

Location:

Phone:

Fax:

E-mail:

FIGURE 6.8 Sample Media Fact Sheet: Television Station

Name of Station:

Affiliation: For example, ABC, NBC, CBS, PBS, FOX or local independent

News Broadcast Schedule: What times of day does this station air local news?

Service Area: How far does this television station's signal reach?

Public Affairs or Interview Programs: List any programs that might be places for library staff or other supporters participate. Be sure to include the contact person for each program.

PSA Submission Lead Times: How far in advance do they need to receive PSAs?

PSA Submission Requirements: Call and ask. They will tell you details such as the maximum length that they accept. Ask if they accept prerecorded video public service announcements.

Staff/Work Hours/Topics Covered/Best Time to Contact: List your contacts here. Find out the best time to call them and what topics they might be interested in.

Mailing Address:

Location:

Phone:

Fax:

E-mail:

FIGURE 6.9 Sample Media Fact Sheet: Radio Station

Name of Station:

Format: For example, talk, country, rock, classics, Christian

Target Audience: What age range does this radio station try to attract?

Service Area: How far does this radio station's signal reach?

Public Affairs or Interview Programs: List any programs that might be places for library staff or other supporters participate. Be sure to include the contact person for each program.

PSA Submission Lead Times: How far in advance do they need to receive PSAs?

PSA Submission Requirements: Call and ask. They will tell you details such as the maximum length that they accept. Ask if they accept prerecorded public service announcements.

Staff/Work Hours/Topics Covered/Best Time to Contact: List your contacts here. Find out the best time to call them and what topics they might be interested in.

Mailing Address:

Location:

Phone:

Fax:

E-mail:

derful feature story on the 11 o'clock news, but it isn't going to preempt a plane crash. There are, however, always slow news days. So, part of your job is to develop a list of stories to keep in your desk drawer—"stories in the drawer"—for such occasions. Draft a couple of notes about the angle for your story, who should be interviewed, and so forth. As you build a relationship with various reporters, hint that you keep a file of potential stories. Tell them a little bit about one or two of them. Eventually you will get a call from a reporter who is looking for news and you'll be able to say, "I have the following stories that you might be interested in using. What can I do to help you?"

If you are a school library media specialist or an academic librarian, you might want to use this technique to sell stories to your district, college, or university communications office. Draft your ideas and send them to the communications office on a regular basis. Let them know that something newsworthy is always happening in your library.

Keeping stories in the drawer is an excellent way to get feature coverage, and once a reporter knows that you can come through in a pinch with a good feature, you will get more calls from both the reporter and his or her editor—when they are hard up to fill the 6 o'clock news or the features page of the newspaper.

DEALING WITH BAD NEWS OR A CRISIS

The following story describes the dilemma faced by anyone who has to deliver bad news.

> Allan went away for six months and left his cat with his younger brother Sam. After about a week, Allan called Sam and asked about the cat. Sam said, "Sorry, Allan, the cat fell of the roof and died." Allan was devastated, but after he composed himself, he told his brother, "Sam, that was a terrible way to tell me that. You should have told me in stages. One time, when I called you could have said the cat is up on the roof and he won't come down. And the next time, you could have told me he fell and was seriously injured. And then the next time, it would have been okay to tell me he was dead." Sam thoughtfully said okay and they continued to chat for a while. Finally, Allan asked, "How's Mom?" Sam responded, "Mom's up on the roof and she won't come down."
>
> The moral is: There is no good way to tell bad news!

Be forthright. Tell the whole story as much as you can share. If there has been a bomb threat and that is why your building has been evacuated, tell the reporter just that. If a book is being challenged by the parent of a student in your school and a reporter has been contacted, share the reviews you used in selecting the book with the reporter. Remember that it is always better that they come to *you* for information pertaining to your library. Be honest and frank, and you will ensure that they will return in the future.

In crisis situations, you may want to prepare a written statement for release to the press. You can have it reviewed by the library director, legal counsel, and even the police depending on the situation. By preparing a written statement, you ensure that the same information is released to all media. You may still want to answer specific questions, but when things are hectic because of the nature of a situation, a written statement helps you communicate your message.

You must also be careful not to share information that is legally protected. For example, in most states, you wouldn't allow anyone to have access to your patron database without a court order. Other areas to be careful about are those having to do with negotiations and personnel. If a personnel matter is of interest to the press, consult legal counsel before releasing any information. Find out exactly what you can and can't share, and what you should and shouldn't say. In matters of confidentiality, it is important to be careful about the information that you release.

A crisis situation for your library can be turned into a positive media opportunity. For example, if you have a fire at one of your branch libraries, the press might be interested in doing a follow-up story on the neighborhood volunteers who helped you with clean-up. A television station might want to feature the heroic efforts of a library staff person who performed CPR on the man who had a heart attack in the stacks. After a story on the series of purse-snatchings at your library, you might be able to convince a reporter to do a follow-up story on the new security measures, urging patrons not to leave their belongings unattended. Every crisis, every challenge can be a positive opportunity for your library when it comes to telling your story.

OTHER OPPORTUNITIES FOR WORKING WITH THE LOCAL MEDIA

There may be other opportunities for working with your local newspaper, television stations, and radio stations. They probably all have public affairs divisions that produce programs and projects that your school, public, or academic library could support. For example, when you see an advertisement for an upcoming public affairs television program on alcoholism, call the station and ask to speak to the public affairs director. Say that your library would be willing to prepare a book list on alcoholism.

The broadcast media offers opportunities for coverage that don't exist in the print world. Television talk shows and radio call-in shows are wonderful chances to tell your library's story. If your local television station has a regular talk show, you might try to schedule library staff or individuals who are presenting programs at the library to appear on the show. This is a great chance to tell the library's story in more than a 30-second sound bite. Be sure that the people you send are confident and articulate, and brief them on what they will be discussing before they arrive in the studio. Radio call-in shows can also be a great tool for spreading your message if you carefully select the person who represents your library. Make sure that the library representative knows and understands the discussion topic and can think of his or her feet. If it is your representative's first experience with such an interview, consider rehearsing together beforehand and have him or her listen to the show several times before the appearance. Listening to the show will indicate what the interviewer is like and what kind of people call with questions.

Many newspapers have a Newspapers In Education program and might like to work with school and public librarians as they develop their materials for distribution to teachers and students. Such a program is also part of relationship building with the media and can help you promote your services and resources.

A Note About Library Press

By all means, send the occasional release about a successful program or service to the national library press. In fact, include a color or black-and-white photo if you have a particularly good one from your National Library Week celebration or new building opening. As you know from browsing these publications, they do run these items and it helps create a national profile for your library. In addition, you will be able to show your library board, school board members, or members of your city council that your efforts merits national recognition. Do not, however, put the national library press on your mailing list for every single news release that you send out; it is a waste of time and money for you and after a while they will dismiss an envelope from your library as just another holiday closing—even though it might be an exciting story about a unique program at your library. Target the releases and photos that you send to the library press just as you do to your local press.

KEEPING TRACK OF MEDIA COVERAGE

You've worked hard to get the local media to cover your library's activities and you have been successful. But your work is far from over! First, you must work to maintain the relationships you have developed. Second, it is important to keep track of and analyze the coverage you have received.

Make a regular practice of scanning all local print publications for articles mentioning your library. Clip them and store them, by topic, in a file or a scrapbook. Take note of who the reporter is, which library staff are quoted, the length of the articles, and so forth. In addition, monitor radio and television broadcasts, and make video and audio tapes of coverage of your library. Mark the tapes with the date, topic, and station for each story, and store them in one place—so you review them when you create your next public relations/communications plan or when you assess the progress of achieving the goal in your current plan. You are creating an archive of the media coverage of your library. This archive will be an invaluable resource when you audit your communications efforts, consider future communications efforts, or need to show your library board that your library is, in fact, getting lots of coverage from the local media.

CABLE-ACCESS PROGRAMS

Developing cable-access programming for your library may not really be media coverage, but it is an opportunity to share your library's story using television, but with the ability to shape the message yourself rather than having a reporter put a specific "spin" on it. Most school, public, and academic libraries have opportunities to produce and air cable-access programs. In fact, many school districts, cities, and universities have their own cable channels and are often desperately seeking quality programming.

Developing and producing your own cable-access program is a time-consuming task. Even if the production expenses are provided by the cable channel, you need to think about focus, talent, and script. A program with an amateur appearance may communicate the wrong message about your library and be worse than not having any cable television presence. Finding quality talent for your program may also be a challenge. Some libraries, however, have been successful at developing a talk-show format that focuses on their programs and services. If you have the time and energy and can find the talent to do this, it can be a wonderful way to disseminate accurate information about your library.

Another option is to produce one or two programs on an annual basis that provide an overview of your library or focus on a couple of services. You can put resources into developing these "feature" programs and then ask the channel to air them on a revolving basis. If you choose this option, be sure not to include any time-sensitive information in your programs, so that they can have a relatively long life. For example, if you produce a program on your school library's services and resources, you can mention that you host parents nights on a regular basis, but don't mention dates.

The least time-intensive option for producing cable-access programming is taping and airing library programs (for example, a preschool storytime or an adult program). You provide the public with a preview of what they could take advantage of if they visited your library, and yet you don't have to plan, cast, or script each program. Be careful to select programs that would air well on television. For example, a book discussion group may not be the best choice because participants might be nervous and there may be lags in the discussion. Presentation programs, such as a reading by a local author, are probably better options. Remember, however, that you may have no control over when these programs air—you may find preschool storytime is being shown at 2 a.m. on occasion!

Cable access can be an inexpensive and effective way to tell your library's story, particularly if you have free access to production facilities and staff. Best of all, your programs will probably air over and over again. Granted, sometimes it will be in the middle of the night, but a program about your library may be a viable alternative for insomniacs whose only other television choices are "infomercials."

HAVE FUN!

Working with the media takes a lot of effort, but it can be highly rewarding and you will get to know some wonderful people. It is impossible to put a dollar value on the kind of assistance these people can give you in telling your story and in creating a positive public perception of your library. Working with reporters to present your library in a positive light and helping them to produce interesting and informative news stories can be a really enjoyable experience. Have fun!

7 TELLING YOUR STORY THROUGH VOLUNTEERS

People are the best public relations tool available, and using volunteers in your library can help you get the job done and tell your story. In fact, there is no better way to tell your story than to ask people to become a part of it! But you have to recruit, train, and reward volunteers before they will be a positive public relations tool for your library. As with all communications tools, managing volunteers requires both human and fiscal resources and—if they are not handled thoughtfully and carefully—they can do more harm than good in terms of creating a positive public perception of your library. A professionally managed volunteer program, however, will attract high-quality volunteers who will become community missionaries for your library.

The key to using volunteers successfully is to treat them like paid employees. In *The Pursuit of WOW!* Tom Peters says, "Never treat a temp like a temp!" The same goes for volunteers. To paraphrase Peters, treat volunteers just as you would paid employees—welcome them into your library, show them respect and trust, give them real responsibilities, and hold them to the same high standards.[1]

The guidelines for making effective use of volunteers that follow are only the tip of the iceberg. Designing and implementing an effective volunteer program is complex and important work. If you decide that a volunteer program may help your library meet its public relations and/or service goals, you may wish to consult *Recruiting and Managing Volunteers in Libraries: A How-to-Do-It Manual*, (Neal-Schuman, 1995) by Bonnie F. McCune and Charleszine Nelson, for more in-depth information.

DEVELOPING YOUR VOLUNTEER PROGRAM

Volunteers can provide additional human resources for your library and they can also be highly effective public relations tools. They are members of the community who think that your library and services are valuable enough that they contribute their time and energy to providing them. That commitment communicates a great deal even before they tell their friends and relatives about the library's programs and services. The effectiveness of your library's volunteers as spokespersons for your library, however, is dependent upon the effective management of your volunteer program. In addition, remember that a well-managed volunteer program communicates to the community that your library is well-managed—even to those individuals who never have the time or the inclination to volunteer.

Whether your library needs one volunteer or several hundred, you will want to develop a volunteer program that includes job descriptions, recruitment strategies, training, and opportunities to recognize and reward your volunteers. In many ways, volunteers should be treated as "unpaid employees." They should be as involved in the life of your library as your paid employees and you should put as much time and energy into their selection and training as you do for your paid employees. In the end, the time that you invest in your library's volunteers will pay off with well-trained, committed, unpaid employees and wonderful community spokespeople for your library.

MAKE SURE THERE IS WORK

Before you decide to recruit volunteers for your library, make sure you have something for them to do. If you are in a school library, they may be able to help with shelving or processing books or with cutting out figures for your library's bulletin boards. In a public library, you may want volunteers to serve as docents and give tours of your library or to train patrons in how to use the online catalog or your Internet services. Perhaps your library has a literacy program and needs volunteers to teach reading to English-as-a-second-language students.

Once you decide that there are jobs for volunteers, write volunteer job descriptions just as you would for a paid position. Include a description of the work, who the position reports to, a work schedule, and the type of training, education, or skills that the job requires. Decide how many positions you have open in each job description area. These descriptions will help you recruit volunteers. When someone calls and asks about the volunteer opportunity you are promoting, you will be able to give them specific details about the position. Do not start recruiting volunteers until you have job descriptions—that would not be a positive experience for your recruits and could be a negative public relations move for your library. Sample job descriptions appear in Figures 7.1 and 7.2.

It is also a good idea to determine a minimum amount of time that a volunteer must commit to the position. Training volun-

FIGURE 7.1 Sample Job Description

Parent Volunteer: School Library Media Center

This parent volunteer will provide support for the Library Media Specialist. The position includes opportunities to work with students, teachers, and other parents, using library materials and computers.

Duties:

- Mend books and magazines
- Shelve books
- Assist in selection of materials for the library media center's parent collection
- Assist students in checking out materials
- Prepare new materials for circulation
- Assist students in using materials and equipment
- Develop artwork for library media center bulletin boards

Qualifications: Enthusiasm; manual dexterity; desire to work with students, teachers, and other parents. Some knowledge of how to use computer is helpful.

Supervisor: Library Media Specialist

Schedule: Monday, Wednesday, and Friday
11 a.m.–2 p.m.

To apply, visit the library media center, Monday through Friday, 3 to 4 p.m., or call the Library Media Specialist at 555–5555.

FIGURE 7.2 Sample Job Description

Children's Room Volunteers (3 positions)

Anytown Public Library

These volunteer positions support the Children's Librarian. Each offers opportunities for working with children and parents, using children's library materials. Volunteers also assist in the development of the library's summer reading program.

Duties:

- Prepare seasonal displays of children's materials
- Assist children and parents in selecting library materials
- Mend children's books and magazines
- Shelve children's books
- Assist Children's Librarian in program planning and presentation
- Assist children and parents in using materials and computers, including the Internet
- Assist Children's Librarian in developing booklists, promotional materials, and programs for the summer reading program

Qualifications: Enthusiasm, manual dexterity, desire to work with children, knowledge of how to use a computer and the Internet. Some knowledge of children's literature is helpful.

Supervisor: Children's Librarian

Schedules: Monday and Wednesday

noon–3 p.m.

Tuesday and Thursday

noon–3 p.m.

Wednesday and Saturday

1–4 p.m.

To apply, contact the Anytown Public Library Volunteer Coordinator (415-777-7777), Monday through Friday, 10 a.m. to 4 p.m.

teers takes library resources, so you want volunteers to stay long enough for your investment to pay off. For example, you may want at least a two-year commitment from your docents. In contrast, you may need only a short commitment from the parent who is helping with your bulletin boards. You may also have some project-based volunteer opportunities. For example, you might need a group of volunteers to run your library's annual book sale—to come in for a specific period of time, do their work, and go away until the next time you are ready for a sale.

MAKE SURE THE WORK IS MEANINGFUL

After you read the job description, think about whether or not you would consider volunteering your time for this position. Is the work meaningful? Will it make the volunteer feel that he or she is truly contributing something to the library? Recruiting volunteers to come into the library every week and do nothing more than put pockets in new books might not be an easy task. You might want to incorporate such a job into a broader job description that includes opportunities for working with other library staff or volunteers or that includes some other interaction with people. For example, parent volunteers at the school library might find helping to process books more bearable if they occasionally could use their creativity to help with bulletin boards.

If you advertise higher-level tasks, you will recruit higher-level volunteers. Many retired people with high levels of education and excellent skills are looking for meaningful volunteer opportunities. Think about those things your library would do if you could only afford it and then match those tasks with qualified and interested volunteers!

Providing volunteers with meaningful work will make the experience rewarding for them. They will tell their friends, relatives, and neighbors about the contribution they are making, and, at the same time, they will tell about the valuable services and programs that your library is providing.

One note: If you are in a library with a union, you may want to confirm that you are not recruiting volunteers for negotiated tasks. Often, union leaders are willing to approve recruitment of volunteers particularly for tasks that library staff don't want to do or don't have time to do. Unions can be understanding about fiscal restraints and the importance of using volunteers in libraries, but checking first is the best strategy.

RECRUITING AND RETAINING VOLUNTEERS

As for other parts of your public relations/communications program, one person will need to be responsible for coordinating the recruitment, training, and management of your volunteer staff. This doesn't mean that person has to do all the work, but one person should coordinate your library's efforts so that no enthusiastic and willing volunteer falls between the cracks.

Once your volunteer job descriptions are written, you are ready to recruit volunteers to fill the positions. You have a variety of options for promoting the opportunities. You may want to run a notice in your newsletter. If you are in a school, you could send a notice home with students or ask the PTO president if he or she knows of any parents who might be interested. Call the local senior citizens center and find out if they have a volunteer coordinator or if you can post your positions on their bulletin board. List your positions with a local volunteer coordinating agency. Maybe the local government television station will run your announcement along with the paid positions that they regularly advertise. You may also want to write a news release announcing the positions and distribute it via the local media. Just as with a paid position, you may want to specify an application deadline for your volunteer positions to facilitate scheduling interviews.

The Challenge of Recruiting Volunteers Today

There are challenges to recruiting volunteers today! The economic necessity for two-income households has put many individuals into the paid workforce who would otherwise have spent their time as volunteers. Evening and weekend hours that might be spent on volunteer work are dedicated to errands and other family duties that don't get done during the hectic work week. This is another reason that it is critical that volunteer work be meaningful and valued.

The opportunity to volunteer in your school library may provide parents with the chance to give something back to the school and also to observe what is happening where their children spend much of their time. A grandmother who misses her grandchildren in another city values helping with preschool storytime. Helping patrons use your special history collections provides the stressed-out banker with a chance to use his undergraduate history degree and a distraction from his daily grind of numbers and balance sheets.

The example of the banker above expresses an important point. When recruiting volunteers for your library, don't assume that people will want to do the same thing in your library that they do every day for pay. The public relations person from the local hospital may not want or be able to help your library with its public relations efforts, but that person might enjoy serving as a docent or helping to process books. In general, people who have full-time jobs do volunteer work for relaxation rather than as an extension of their work day. In addition, for conflict of interest reasons, they may not be able to help your library in their area of expertise. Don't assume automatically that a lawyer will want to volunteer legal services; a banker financial advice; or a public relations person assistance with your library's public relations. Ask them about their interests and you may find they have much to offer in other areas.

Applications and Interviews

If volunteers have to apply for your positions, they will know that you are serious about the jobs that need to be done and the kind of people you need to do them. Set up a formal application and interview process for volunteer positions, just like the process for a paid position. Ask careful questions and then choose the volunteer who is best for the job.

Possible volunteer interview questions might include

Why did you apply for this volunteer position at our library?
Tell me about your other volunteer experiences.
Do you have any questions about the job description?
Can you work the schedule outlined in the job description?
Are you willing to make the time commitment described in the job description?

You will also want to ask specific questions about the applicant's skills, education, and experience in the areas specified in the job description. Do this just as if you were hiring a paid employee.

Tell me about your experience working with computers.
What special skills, experiences or education do you have that would help you serve as a docent for our library?

Training and Supervision

Like any library employee, volunteers require training and supervision. Be sure that a supervisor is assigned to any volunteer who works in your library; the volunteer has someone to go to with questions or problems and the supervisor can monitor the volunteer's work and make sure that the volunteer is having a positive experience at your library.

Volunteers should also receive training and orientation similar to that provided for paid employees. In addition to training in the specific tasks of the volunteer position, a tour of the library, the opportunity to meet all of the employees and see all of the service areas, and a review of the library's policies and procedures should be part of each volunteer's orientation and training. If you are recruiting a corps of volunteers or several volunteers for one task, you may want to offer orientation and/or training on a regular basis each month. Or you might want to include volunteers in part of your regularly scheduled employee orientation sessions. The important thing is to provide your volunteers with all of the information they need to complete their tasks successfully and so that they feel as if they are a part of your library's staff.

Time Sheets

Volunteers should complete and file time sheets just like paid employees. In some cases, you will be required to pay insurance for volunteers who work in your library and you will need these records to compute your rates. In addition, these records provide helpful information when you want, for example, to reward your volunteers for their hours of service or when you need to counsel a volunteer who consistently does not show up for the scheduled hours.

Personnel Files

You should keep a file, similar to the personnel file you keep for paid employees, for each of your volunteers. In the file, you should keep the volunteer's application, the job description for the volunteer position, and copies of all time sheets. In addition, this is a good place to put copies of letters of recognition that you have sent to the volunteer and notes about things that you want to praise the volunteer for, such as the wonderful way that she helped a small child find his mother when he was lost after storytime.

This file is also the place to keep copies of any official documents, such as insurance release forms, that your organization requires your volunteers to sign. A form listing whom to contact in an emergency is another good piece of information to have in the volunteer's file. This is the personnel file for your volunteer and, just as for paid employees, you will find it valuable to have this information organized and readily available.

Reviews

You will want to be sure that either you or each volunteer's supervisor schedules regular review sessions with each volunteer. These sessions, held every three or six months, are a formal opportunity for the volunteer to share any questions or problems that he or she may have and for the supervisor to provide the volunteer with positive feedback and constructive criticism.

Telling a volunteer that he can improve the way he completes his duties does not have to be a negative experience. First of all, it tells the volunteer that someone cares about what he is doing. Second, if the supervisor uses positive language and talks about improvement, the suggestion will be viewed as positive. However, if it is clear that the job assigned is not the best place for the volunteer, it may be the supervisor's responsibility to counsel the volunteer about finding a new assignment in the library.

Consider the volunteer who has been gluing pockets in books, but the pockets are crooked because she doesn't have the manual dexterity to complete the task. The supervisor may have noticed that she has a wonderful relationship with the small children who visit the library. So, perhaps a better assignment for her is as an assistant at preschool storytime. Chances are that both the library staff and the volunteer will be happier if this change is made. While volunteers should be treated like paid employees in many ways, you often have more freedom to change the job assignments for volunteers than for paid employees.

Recognition and Rewards

Buy your volunteers name badges like those paid staff wear. List their name and title, *Volunteer*. Invite them to your staff parties, staff meetings, and special events. Once a volunteer comes on board, he or she is part of your internal audience.

Remember, however, that volunteers are donating their time to your library. Recognition is the only reward they get. Publish their names in your newsletter often. Recognize the number of hours they have donated at an annual "Volunteer Recognition Ceremony"; such a ceremony is a great opportunity for a media event. Send your volunteers to your state library association conference so they can network with other library volunteers. Be sure they get several thank-you letters each year. When you walk through the library, remember to stop by volunteers' workstations and say "thanks." Encourage the library director, building principal, or board chair to do the same. Volunteers are contributing something very special to your library. If they know how much you appreciate their contribution you can be sure they'll tell their friends and neighbors what a special place your library is and how important it is to the community.

CHILDREN AND TEENS AS VOLUNTEERS

Children and teenagers can be dedicated, hardworking volunteers. They want to help, learn, and feel that they are contributing. Just as for adult volunteers, it is important that you identify appropriate and meaningful tasks for these volunteers.

The Young Adult Library Services Association (YALSA), a division of the American Library Association, advocates meaningful opportunities for youths to volunteer. In its manual, *Youth Participation in School and Public Libraries: It Works*, YALSA provides guidelines for youth volunteerism or "youth participation" in libraries. Youth participation is defined as the "involvement of young adults in responsible action and significant decision-making which affects the design and delivery of library and information services for their peers and their communities."[2] The result of this participation is, according to YALSA, "more responsible and effective library and information services for this age group" and enhanced "learning, personal development, citizenship and transition to adulthood" for the teenagers.[3]

In addition, YALSA suggests that projects involving youths should have the following characteristics:

- be centered on issues of real interest and concern to youth
- have the potential to benefit people other than those directly involved
- allow for youth input from the planning stage forward
- focus on some specific, doable tasks
- receive adult support and guidance, but avoid adult domination
- allow for learning and development of leadership and group work skills
- contain opportunities for training and for discussion of progress made and problems encountered
- give evidence of youth decisions being implemented
- avoid exploitation of youth for work which benefits the agency rather than the young adults
- seek to recruit new participants on a regular basis
- plan for staff time, funds, administrative support, transportation, etc., before launching project
- show promise of becoming an ongoing, long term activity.[4]

While many of these characteristics are the same as those recommended for adult volunteer opportunities, the list also includes special consideration for the needs of youths. Above all, YALSA reminds us that youth volunteers should both contribute and receive benefit from their volunteer work. They should not be exploited simply as "free labor," but should be respected, listened to, and have opportunities for learning on the job.

PARENT VOLUNTEERS IN SCHOOL LIBRARIES

If you are in a school library, you may have access to your building or district's corps of volunteers. You may only need to develop job descriptions and submit them to the volunteer coordinator to find the help you are seeking. Schools also have a wonderful pool of potential volunteers in the parents, guardians, and grandparents of their students. Often these individuals want to be involved in the life of their child's school, and volunteering in the library is an excellent way for them to do this.

Best of all, parents who volunteer in the school library media center will learn about what happens there and the value of the program. They can become advocates for the program. Showing people something is a good way to communicate your message—involving them in it is the best way!

A school librarian may also have tasks, such as preparing art for the bulletin board or desktop-publishing bookmarks or flyers for the students, that a parent can do at home. Such tasks allow parents to contribute without having to rearrange their work schedules to be at school during the day.

Parent organizations, such as PTAs and PTOs, are excellent sources of volunteers for school libraries. Often the parents involved in this group are looking for opportunities to contribute to the school on a regular or project basis. When you determine your volunteer needs, approach your school's parent organization and ask for their help. They may offer to come in on a Saturday as a large group to help move your library, rather than have you recruit two people to do it over a period of two weeks. Seek their assistance in getting the job done and you'll be amazed at the end result!

VOLUNTEER SPEAKERS BUREAUS

Perhaps one of the strategies in your public relations/communications plan is to make presentations about your library and its services to a variety of community groups. When you are ready to implement this strategy, however, you may discover that library staff aren't available to leave the library to make these presentations. Developing a volunteer speakers bureau may be the way to implement your strategy.

A speakers bureau is an excellent way to spread the word about your library—and who could be better to go out and tell the story than community members? You may wish to train a group of volunteers to be a part of your library's speakers bureau. For example, the mother of a handicapped child who has used your resources since the child's birth might tell you that she would love to volunteer, but she simply can't adhere to a regular schedule. She would be a wonderful member of the speakers bureau, telling your library's story from her own point of view; after the initial training she could schedule speaking engagements as they fit into her schedule. Best of all, you have a wonderful missionary telling your story and you don't have to leave a library service desk unattended.

You will want to provide speakers bureau volunteers with a draft presentation script and lots of resources, such as handouts. It also might be a good idea to offer to videotape a rehearsal of their presentations for a critique of their style—perhaps a speech professor from a local college or university would be willing to review these tapes for your volunteers. You will probably also want to coordinate scheduling the speakers through your library so that you can make good matches. For example, the retired small businessman who can talk about how your library's business collection helped him build his business is probably the best speaker for the Chamber of Commerce's business forum. By having requests come to the library, you can contact your speakers and make the matches.

Do consider using volunteers as part of a speakers bureau. It will give you the opportunity to recruit volunteers who are willing to donate their time, but have difficulty adhering to a regular schedule. It also offers you a way to answer those requests for a Rotary Club speaker without having to rearrange staff schedules or close a service desk.

FRIENDS OF THE LIBRARY

All libraries need "friends"! Friends groups began in the 1920s and 1930s at libraries at such universities as Yale, Harvard, Princeton, and Columbia, and moved into public libraries as they were established.[5] A Friends group can complement your volunteer program. Members of the Friends of the Library are not only volunteers, they are designated advocates for your library and for library service.

Friends of the Library groups serve libraries in several primary ways. They assist in the planning, funding, and promotion of library programming, and they are library fundraisers. Often their fundraising activities center around used book sales.

Friends usually have a separate corporate structure from the library, by incorporating as a nonprofit organization. They have their own officers and bylaws, and, working with a library liaison, they make their own decisions. Friends may have more discretion about how they spend their money than the library has. For example, you may not be able to spend money from your

---

Facts About Friends

- More than half of all Friends groups have between 100 and 500 members.

- More than 38 percent of Friends organizations are less than 10 years old.

- The mean amount of money raised in fiscal year 1993 by Friends groups was $23,402; the median amount was $6,235. Most of the funds raised by Friends was used for non-capital projects; only 17 percent was donated to capital campaigns. More than 60 percent of all Friends groups have not solicited corporate donations.

—*From a 1994 Friends of Libraries USA survey of 600 Friends groups.*[6]

library's budget to hold a reception during National Library Week, but the Friends can spend their money to plan and host a reception. The reception is an opportunity for the Friends to promote membership in their organization and to invite city leaders to enjoy the refreshments and learn more about the valuable services the library provides in your community. You can hold the reception in the library and promote it together. One event helps both you and the Friends achieve your respective goals.

Having an active Friends of the Library group is important on a day-to-day basis, but it becomes critical when your library is campaigning for a bond issue or a levy increase or when you face a serious intellectual freedom challenge. The Friends become your citizen advocates—they are spokespeople for your cause without the vested interest that some people might attribute to library staff.

When you develop your library's public relations plan, you should consider whether or not you need Friends of the Library to reach your goal. Ask such questions as

- What parts of our public relations plan will be difficult to achieve without assistance from individuals outside the library staff? Could a Friends group provide this assistance?
- What components of our public relations plan require advocacy in the community? Could members of a Friends of the Library group play that role in the community?

Once you formulate answers to these questions, your next step will be to identify someone in your community to organize a Friends group. Think about approaching a library trustee or dedicated volunteer and proposing the idea. These individuals already have an understanding of the goals and objectives of your library, and they are also probably well connected in your community.

As with any part of your public relations program, don't wait until you are in a crisis situation to decide you need "friends."

FOLUSA

When you are ready to organize a Friends group for your library, you may wish to contact Friends of Libraries USA (FOLUSA) for information. This national organization defines its mission as "dedicated to motivating and supporting the efforts of your local Friends group." It is a coalition of more than 2,800 Friends groups throughout the country. FOLUSA's newsletter, *News Update*, and fact sheets such as "How to Organize a Friends Group" will provide you with valuable information as you begin your organizing efforts.

For more information about FOLUSA membership, contact Friends of Libraries USA, 1700 Walnut, #715, Philadelphia, PA 19103, (215) 790–1674.

COMMUNITY ORGANIZATIONS

A big project, such as painting the children's room or putting security strips in all of your books, may be the perfect community service project for a local service club like the Rotary Club or Kiwanis. Such projects have a beginning and an end and can usually be accomplished in a matter of days by a large number of people working together. Think about approaching a local service club when you have a project like this to accomplish. Groups like these are always looking for projects that will contribute to the community and increase their public profile.

Involving community groups in library projects will often encourage additional media coverage of your library. The local newspaper will be enthusiastic about running a photograph of the mayor and Rotary Club members painting the children's room. And the Rotary Club may publish an article about the project in their newsletter, spreading the word to another audience.

INTERNS FROM COLLEGES AND UNIVERSITIES

When your library has a special project for which you need volunteer help, you might want to recruit interns from local colleges or universities. Managing the promotion for your summer reading program might be the perfect opportunity for a public relations major. Setting up the books for your new Friends of the Library group might be a great special project for an accounting major. Students may choose to work for your library as an internship for college credit. You may even set up relationships with university faculty that will provide you with student interns on a regular basis. By working with the faculty at the university, you can be sure that the volunteers' work will have expert review. You provide students with an opportunity for real work experience in their field and your library gets expert assistance that it otherwise might not be able to afford.

VOLUNTEERS BECOME COMMUNITY REPRESENTATIVES

Your highly valued volunteers will not only contribute to your library in terms of the services they provide; they will also become effective community representatives for your library. As Peter Drucker said of volunteers in *Managing the Nonprofit Organization: Principles and Practice*, "They live in the community and they exemplify the institution's mission. Effective non-profits train their volunteers to represent them in the community."[7]

By developing a comprehensive volunteer program that has a direct relationship to your public relations/communications goals, you will develop volunteers who are able to tell your library's story. The result should mirror the experience that Drucker describes, "Again and again when I talk to volunteers in non-profits, I ask, Why are you willing to give all this time when you are already working hard in your paid job? And again and again I get the same answer, Because here I know what I am doing. Here I contribute. Here I am a member of the community."[8]

NOTES

1. Tom Peters, *The Pursuit of WOW! Every Person's Guide to Topsy-Turvy Times* (New York: Random House, 1994), 67.
2. Young Adult Library Services Association, *Youth Participation in School and Public Libraries: It Works.* (Chicago: American Library Association, 1995), 5.
3. Ibid, 5.
4. Ibid, 5.
5. Anne F. Roberts and Susan Griswold Blandy, *Public Relations for Librarians* (Englewood, Colorado: Libraries Unlimited, 1989), 81.
6. Friends of Libraries USA, *News Update*, 18 (Spring 1996), 1.
7. Peter F. Drucker, *Managing the Nonprofit Organization: Principles and Practices* (New York: HarperCollins, 1990), 161.
8. Drucker, xvii.

8 COMMUNITY INVOLVEMENT AS A PUBLIC RELATIONS TOOL

Your library is a part of many different communities regardless of whether you are in a school, public, or academic library. A public library is part of a city or a county. Branch libraries are part of the neighborhood communities in which they are located. School libraries are members of their building and district-level communities and of the overall neighborhood and city or county that the school serves. Academic libraries are part of their university or college community, the neighborhood that they share with local residents, and their home town or city. Involvement in these communities by your library as an organization and by your library's employees as individuals can be powerful public relations tools for your library. This involvement demonstrates the role that your library plays in the community and provides you and your staff with many opportunities to show how your library contributes to the community.

In addition, if public relations is truly about creating positive public perception, the relationship your library staff builds with other members of the community is the most effective tool for developing such positive perceptions. When an employee of your library goes home in the evening, stands in his backyard, and talks about your library in a positive way to his "neighbor over the fence," that is the best public relations available—and it can be both the most expensive and inexpensive tool to buy.

Let's face it. If library staff don't speak positively in the community about your library, how can you expect your volunteers to talk about why your library is important? And, ultimately, how can you expect the community to perceive your library as a "community value," if even the people who feed their families by working there are dissatisfied by the services provided?

LIBRARY STAFF MEMBERS AS COMMUNITY VOLUNTEERS

Just as community volunteers who come into your library help you achieve your public relations goals, sending library staff out into the community as volunteers will also further your efforts. The library staff person who gets involved as a Little League coach or Rotary member or who is in charge of the town's annual fun-run to benefit muscular dystrophy is giving something back to the community. Such a contribution reflects both on the person involved and on the organization he or she works for, especially if the organization—your library—supports the involvement.

Described in the for-profit sector as "corporate social responsibility," providing support for employees' volunteer efforts is becoming more and more widespread in the 1990s. Sometimes this support is provided by supporting "release time"—allowing employees to do community service as part of their regular work day, without losing pay.

The minute libraries think about sending staff into the community, however, red flags about "time off the desk" and "time away from serving the public" go up. But if public relations is truly a priority for your library, you will need to think creatively about staffing and scheduling to accommodate such involvement. One caveat is necessary—while it is important for library staff to be involved in the community in order to spread the word about your library and its services, staff are still needed in the building to serve the public when they show up to partake of those wonderful services you have been promoting.

A library truly committed to community involvement of its staff might even make it part of the performance appraisal process. In that way, each staff person could work with his or her supervisor to negotiate a way to be involved in the community and for the necessary resources. Sometimes the resource might be time away from the library; at other times employees might be involved on their own time, but the library might pay all or part of an organizational membership fee. The key is for the involvement to be something that the staff member is interested in and something that will provide the person with the opportunity to tell the library story.

Your library might even want to develop an application for community involvement support like that shown in Figure 8.1. This application helps staff define and articulate the type of support they would like the library to provide, and it gives the li-

FIGURE 8.1 Sample Staff Application for Community Involvement Support

Middletown Public Library
Staff Application for Community Involvement Support

Name _____

Position _____

Work schedule _____

Describe the type of community project/volunteer work that you are involved in

_____

_____

What type of support are you seeking (e.g., release time, use of library equipment or supplies, permission to solicit contributions from colleagues on site, reimbursement of membership dues)? _____

_____

_____

For what period of time do you need this support? _____

Why should Middletown Public Library support your involvement?

_____

_____

_____

Signature _____ Date _____

Supervisor's recommendation _____

_____

_____

_____

Supervisor's signature _____ Date _____

Library Director's decision _____

_____

_____

Library Director's signature _____ Date _____

brary a formal way of deciding about the feasibility of such support. For example, without an application process, a staff person who would like to help deliver Meals-On-Wheels to the elderly twice per month might not even consider volunteering—she would need an extra 30 minutes added to her lunch hour each delivery day. If she knows that a mechanism is in place for asking the library to support her involvement, she is more likely to pursue the opportunity and ask the library for support.

It is also important to remember that all library staff have something to contribute to the community. A master's in library science does not make a person uniquely qualified to tell the library's story in the community; in fact, a support or clerical staff person is sometimes more easily recognized by members of the community than a high-level "professional" librarian, and, therefore, has more recognition value. For example, if your library has a booth at the county fair, community members might be more comfortable approaching the booth if the people working there are the library staff they see on a day-to-day basis (rather than administrative staff whom they never see). In addition, nonusers who visit the library after a positive experience in the booth at the county fair may feel more welcome walking in the door to see the circulation staff member who greeted them at the fair.

Release time is still comparatively rare in the business world, but there are other ways to encourage library staff to become involved in the community. You might want to designate a staff person to seek out opportunities for community involvement and to promote them to your staff. Working the phones for the local public television station during its fund drive is a great opportunity for library staff to volunteer as a team; it is a chance for library staff to volunteer together and people watching the telethon see them there as a group—giving something back. If your staff cannot volunteer because of scheduling difficulties, your library could contribute pizza for volunteers to eat or t-shirts for them to wear during the broadcast; the library gets exposure, the staff develop a sense of team spirit, and the community gets needed work done. It makes a lot of sense.

SENDING LIBRARY STAFF INTO THE COMMUNITY

Once your library's staff is ready and willing to go out into the community and spread the word about your library and its services, there are a wide variety of opportunities to do so. They range from becoming involved as members in groups such as the chamber of commerce and the Rotary to making presentations for community groups to staffing a booth at the county fair. The skills and background necessary for these activities are varied enough that there are opportunities for any library staff member who wants to participate.

Community Groups

People often become involved in group volunteer activities for both the opportunity to make a contribution and for the social interaction. The types of organizations that the staff at your library might be interested in getting involved in include

- civic groups
- business clubs
- professional societies
- hobby clubs
- fraternities and sororities
- religious organizations
- sports and recreation clubs
- advocacy organizations
- auxiliaries and "friends of" organizations
- amateur performing arts companies

Involvement in these groups allows library staff the chance to build a network of community contacts. For example, when the Kiwanis Club is looking for a service project, your head reference librarian who is also a Kiwanis member might suggest that the library needs its children's room painted. Library staff involvement in these groups helps integrate the library and its resources into the community. For example, the staff person who is involved with community theater might offer to prepare a list of related library materials for the show program or he might arrange a display of library materials for the theater lobby on opening night. This kind of community outreach is extremely valuable and can only be achieved through the support of library staff involvement in community organizations.

STAFF AS PRESENTERS

Each year, the local Rotary Club appoints a program chair and each year that individual goes crazy trying to plan informative and entertaining programs for the group's weekly meetings. He spends hours on the telephone trying to pin down speakers, tries to talk all of his friends and relatives into presenting at least one program, and when Aunt Minnie refuses to discuss her button collection at the group's next meeting, he wonders why he ever became a Rotarian to begin with. Your library can help make the program chair's experience more pleasurable and can make him admired and envied by his fellow Rotarians. How? By providing the group, on an annual basis, with a list of library staff who are available to make presentations on a wide variety of topics. Best of all, this "speakers bureau," is an excellent way for you to spread the word about your library and its services. The program chair can use this list to schedule your staff to present at his group's meetings throughout the year. (He will also have the list as a backup resource when Uncle Frank has to have gall bladder surgery and can't talk at next week's meeting about his experiences in the Korean War.)

To develop a speakers' bureau for your library, think about the people on your staff who have particular areas of expertise. What subjects areas is your business reference librarian really up-to-date on? Can the librarian in your local history collection talk about the architecture of downtown buildings? Does your collection development librarian love mysteries and mystery writers? Approach people and ask them if they would be willing to develop a presentation to be included on your list. You may wish to put out a general call for presenters, but be careful—perhaps not all of your volunteers will be good presenters, but if they volunteer, you may feel obligated to use them. Your business reference librarian may really know a lot about business reference materials, but could be deadly as a presenter. However, as part of your library's community involvement component of its public relations plan, you might be able to encourage him to be the library's representative to the chamber of commerce where he would be able to share those resources on a one-to-one basis with his fellow members and come back to the library from each meeting with more information about what is happening in your community.

Ask each presenter to complete a speakers bureau presentation description similar to that in Figure 8.2. This description will help you compile your list of presentations and provide you with a reference tool when people call to request a speaker.

Don't forget presentations about books when you develop your speakers bureau. Service clubs and other groups are always looking for booktalks. If you have staff members who are particularly good at talking about books, be sure to include them on your list. You might have staff who can talk about books on a particular subject or genre, such as the Civil War or science fiction, and others who are well suited to talk about the most recent bestsellers. People associate libraries with books and lots of people are looking for a recommendation for a good book to read. Send your librarians out into the community to do just that!

Once you have a list of presenters and they are ready to go out

FIGURE 8.2 Speakers Bureau Presentation Description

Staff person _____

Presentation topic _____

Brief description of presentation _____

_____

_____

_____

_____

Length of presentation _____

Audiovisual equipment required _____

Intended audience (e.g., adults, children, business people, senior citizens)

_____

Days and times presenter is available _____

_____

Additional information _____

_____

into the community, promote your speakers bureau. In addition to compiling a mailing list of service organizations and mailing information, you might want to run an item in your library's newsletter about the available speakers or to issue a news release describing your new service. Remember that, just as for any service your library provides, the public has to know about your speakers bureau and the speakers available before they can take advantage of it.

PARTICIPATING IN COMMUNITY EVENTS

Any special event or activity that takes place in your community offers an avenue for your library to become involved. The possibilities are endless—booths at community and county fairs, a float in the local parade, puppet shows for children during the restaurant fair—and they all include a chance to tell the library story.

In addition, most groups that host special events are anxious to have groups such as libraries involved and will offer booth or display space free or at a reduced rate. Look at your community and think about the possibilities. Could your school library have a booth at the neighborhood's community center festival to exhibit student work? If you are trying to get the people from the neighborhood to use your academic library, handing out magnets listing library hours might be a great outreach tool at the Octoberfest celebration. The key is to determine where the people are that you want to reach—and then to go there to reach them.

If your library has a bookmobile, this can be a great exhibit on wheels. It is easy to transport, has books on it that people can actually check out, and people love to visit a bookmobile. All you have to do is drive the bookmobile to the event, staff it with a couple of friendly library staff, and wait for the crowd to materialize.

If you are a school librarian, try to find a way to participate in all school events. Be a part of the school community! The library should be open (with students using it) on Parents' Night. If the school has a building-wide festival, be sure that you and the library are a part of it.

Academic libraries should also try to participate in school events and activities. Think carefully about how your library can participate in homecoming or parents weekend. Can the welcoming reception for parents be held in your library's lounge? Should the library have a float in the homecoming parade? There are lots of possibilities for involvement that can further your library's public relations goals, and your staff might even have fun in the process!

CONCLUSION

Community involvement for both your library staff, as individuals, and your library, as an organization, is an excellent tool for reaching your public relations goals. Like other public relations tools, it allows you to select your target audience and to participate in activities and events that will reach that audience. It creates a positive public perception of your library as an organization that "gives something back" to the community and supports its staff in "giving something back," too.

9 CREATING AN ENVIRONMENT THAT SUPPORTS YOUR MESSAGE

The key to the success of your public relations efforts is creating a positive environment for their implementation. Attention to details, such as customer service and image, will help develop an environment that will nurture and further your efforts rather than detract from and contradict them.

All the public relations/communications planning and activities in the world will not help you achieve your goal if your library doesn't provide an environment that is conducive to high-quality service and where library employees feel valued and trusted. The creation of this environment is driven from the top down in any organization. The library director and board must believe in such an environment and must work to create it. The school library media specialist must provide an atmosphere of trust for students and faculty members. Unfortunately, sometimes in libraries the care and protection of materials takes precedence over the importance of the relationship with library users. Therefore, it is important that the internal communications message focus on the importance of the patron and high-quality service.

VALUE YOUR STAFF

If library staff feel valued by the organization, they will extend that feeling to the library's customers. Providing staff with the information necessary to do their jobs, rewarding them for doing their jobs well, and supporting staff when they make decisions will make them feel valued.

PROVIDE INFORMATION

The most important audience for any organization is its internal audience. Library staff members must know what is happening within the entire organization in order to understand their role in the big picture and to answer questions from the public. It helps to remember that most patrons see every staff member as a "librarian" and think that every staff member is intimately familiar with all of the library's operations. Therefore, it is important that staff understand what is happening in other library departments so that they can make appropriate referrals. There is nothing worse, for example, than calling a library to ask a question and being transferred six times, getting four individuals' voice mail messages, and then being cut off. If the first person knows where to send the call, this negative experience can be avoided.

You might wish to consider a print or electronic internal newsletter to help keep staff informed. An internal newsletter published on a regular basis is an excellent way to share information and provides staff with something to refer to when questions arise. It can also serve as a vehicle for explaining complex issues. Regular staff meetings will also help to keep the lines of communication open, particularly if they include an open forum where staff are able to ask questions on any topic. Remember that it is important for library staff to know about anything critical that is happening at your library—before it hits the newspapers. Some libraries implement these communications efforts only during times of crisis, such as budget crunches. However, just like the tools you use with your external publics, your internal communications tools will be more effective during times of crisis if they are already a part of day-to-day life in your library.

PROVIDE REWARDS

Rewarding staff for doing their jobs well is a more complex area. Of course, it would be great if rewards could be in terms of salary increases or bonuses. Often, however, this is not fiscally or organizationally possible, but there are other techniques for rewarding excellence in staff service. Developing and implementing a staff recognition program, such as Employee-of-the-Month, is one way. By recognizing staff and sharing that recognition with library users, through posting a photograph on a bulletin board or adding the employee's name to a plaque, can be a source of great pride for library staff. In addition, allowing staff to explore areas of interest and expertise can often be a reward for exemplary service. If you have a children's librarian who has a particular interest and talent for puppetry, for example, sending her to a puppetry workshop rewards her efforts—and it enhances her skills.

PROVIDE SUPPORT

There is a much-repeated story about the returns policy of Nordstrom's, a store praised for its high level of customer service. As the story goes, a customer brought a pair of whitewall tires into a Nordstrom's store to return them. The sales associate accepted the return and gave the customer a refund. However, Nordstrom's is basically an apparel store—they certainly don't carry tires. The story is often told to demonstrate the high level of customer service that Nordstrom's provides, but it also demonstrates the way that the store supports its sales associates' decisions. It is amazing to think that the sales associate felt supported enough to make that decision. Nordstrom's really stands behind the motto, "Use your own best judgment."

Library staff are also often faced with judgment calls: the small child who has $2 in overdue fines and says that his mom is out of work and there is no way he can get the money; the family who comes in to pay for the $500 in library books that were destroyed when their house burned down; the regular patron who insists that he returned two books that show up as overdue on the library's computer. While there needs to be a chain of command for deciding how to handle such situations, the staff on the front lines also need to be trusted and empowered to make those decisions. And when they do make a decision, they need to be supported—even if you ask them to think about things differently in the future.

The information, rewards, and support that you provide to library staff members will be reflected in their attitude and the quality of their work. They will be willing to go the extra mile—and that "can do" attitude will be consistent with the positive public perception of your library that you are trying to create with your communications efforts.

CUSTOMER SERVICE

> Smile at your customers. Reserve your best parking spaces for them. Answer the phone before the third ring. These tips come from the American Library Association. They're offered not to patrons who run businesses, but to libraries themselves.[1]

This opening paragraph from a September 1995 article in *American Demographics* may hold the key to the survival of libraries as institutions in the age of technology. Let's face it—as technology becomes more and more available and people can access information from their homes, their need for some traditional library services is going to decrease. In addition to providing access to technology, however, librarians help people understand and utilize technology. High-quality customer service is key to staying relevant.

An essential part of providing high-quality customer service is learning what customers want. Corporations invest large quantities of money in market research to learn what their customers want; then they set out, sometimes successfully, to provide it. Libraries may or may not have the resources to conduct this type of research, but unlike corporate executives who work in an office building far away from their potential customers, librarians have the advantage of being in direct contact with their customers on a daily basis. In addition, as members of an overall community, librarians have constant contact with potential customers in other parts of their lives.

Special People

Library staff may ask for photographs of "special people," such as board or city council members or the university president, so that they know who deserves "special treatment." While this request may be well intentioned, fulfilling it can detract from high-quality customer service. If the library staff treats every patron as if he or she is a member of the city council or the university president, everyone will receive "special service."

The old adage says, "What goes around comes around." A column in *The Christian Science Monitor* describes a young school library user in the Seattle area and the relationship that he built with his school librarian, who wrote the article. The boy is described to be like any other student. However, that student was Bill Gates, president of Microsoft Corporation.[2] Today, Gates is one of the nation's leading philanthropic contributors to library programs. Perhaps his positive experiences as a child had some influence over his philanthropic decisions as an adult.

Of course, not every patron who has a positive experience at your library will someday be in a position to contribute millions of dollars. Your patrons are, however, already contributing to the support of your library and its services—as taxpayers they fund your public library, as students their tuition helps fund your academic library. They deserve high-quality service and their experiences with your service will influence their decisions about future funding.

PHYSICAL SURROUNDINGS

The physical environment of your library will also support or detract from your communications efforts. A clean, well-cared-for library looks valued. Chances are that your patrons will treat it with care. A messy environment with unemptied trash cans and worktables littered with books appears unvalued, and will cause patrons to treat the furniture and the rest of the physical environment without much care. If books fall on the floor, why pick them up? The place is already a mess.

Even more important to the atmosphere in any library is the signage. Restrictive signage with lots of negatives—don'ts and no's—will provoke an immediate negative reaction from library users. In an effort to protect the physical environment and protect library materials, libraries have a tendency to use this type of signage. It is important to have clear, effective signage that helps patrons use the library. Shelf signs and directional signage are critical for the independent library user.

When developing wording for any sign, think carefully about the message. Even if what you are trying to communicate is restrictive, you can put it in a positive light. Rather than posting signs that say "No food or drink," post signs that says "Food and drink may be enjoyed in the student lounge." Or in your special collection room, signs that read "Pencils only" are much more positive than "No pens." Yet, in both cases, the messages are exactly the same and they evoke more positive reactions.

Also, watch out for sign pollution. Sometimes in an effort to be helpful and provide lots of information, libraries put up so many signs that patrons are confused. Keep the quantity of signs to a minimum and keep the message simple. Stick with signs that provide direction and use other communications tools, such as brochures and newsletters, to communicate policy and share program and service information.

IMAGE

The bottom line is that public relations is about image! It is about the image that your library projects and, therefore, it is about the image projected by you and by every member of your library's staff. This can be a touchy area to discuss because it is related to people's individual style and behavior. But when your staff carefully consider their personal image and its impact on their job success and the success of the library, they will probably admit that changes—small or large—will help them progress toward their personal goals and help the library progress toward its public relations goals.

A PROFESSION WITH AN IMAGE PROBLEM?

Is librarianship a profession with an image problem? If you read the professional journals and follow the Internet listservs and newsgroups, you would certainly think so. Librarians are constantly talking about the profession's image problem and what the media and advertisers do to perpetuate it. But, let's be frank! Do lawyers have an image problem? Do doctors? Have you heard more insulting jokes in the past year about lawyers or about librarians?

In many ways, librarians and libraries have an image advantage. While comic strips and television shows may sometimes perpetuate the image of the old-lady librarian with a bun and half-glasses and a QUIET sign on the front of her desk, ask anyone you meet on the street how they feel about libraries. Most likely people will tell you a warm, fuzzy story from their childhood or confess to you some deep, dark secret about an overdue book. In general, our society places a positive value on libraries and books, and librarians are in a position to capitalize on that part of our culture. So, don't spend your time behind the desk, complaining about the image of librarians, and, in the end, perpetuating it—get out on the other side, meet and greet the public, and capitalize on the cultural value that our society places on libraries.

DRESS FOR SUCCESS

Dressing for success is important in this society—ask any lawyer preparing a client for court. Tom Peters in his book, *The Pursuit of Wow!* recommends that readers develop their own style and "show care and show confidence."[3] Be sure that the clothes you wear match the task you are completing. A power suit is as inappropriate for moving the library collection as shorts are for a library board meeting. Think carefully about the image your clothes project based on the situation. And, when in doubt, dress up!

People will know that you think what you are doing is important—important enough to take time and care with your appearance.

This may sound trivial, but people will perceive your library in a much more positive light if they see staff who care about their appearance. Patrons will believe that they are in an important place—because the people who work there think it is important.

DEVELOP YOUR COMMUNICATIONS SKILLS

Developing your personal communications skills and helping other library staff to develop their skills will contribute to the success of your public relations efforts. Effective communication is a growing edge for many people and there are lots of resources available for improving those skills. Toastmasters and the Dale Carnegie course are just two options that may be available in your local area. In addition, there may be trainers in your community who can provide ongoing staff development training for your library in the areas of image and communicating effectively.

As you and the staff of your library become more effective communicators, you will find that the job of telling your library's story is a more enjoyable one. Participating in radio and television interviews will be fun and a challenge, instead of a cause of knocking knees and sweaty palms. Even dealing with patrons (particularly the difficult ones) across a public service desk will become an easier task. Improving the communications skills of library staff will ultimately improve another important area that will support your public relations efforts—customer service.

SCAN YOUR SURROUNDINGS

After you have developed your public relations/communications goal, take a walk through your library. Look at the furniture, the paint, the signage, the demeanor of the library staff. Think about all of these environmental influences in terms of the impact that they can have, and consider whether they support or detract from your communications goal. Then, set about changing those that detract from your efforts—and enhancing those that support your efforts. When community members, students, or patrons who have learned about your library decide to visit, they will encounter an environment and people who support the message you have communicated.

NOTES

1. Tibbett L. Speer, "Libraries from A to Z." *American Demographics*, September 1995: 48.
2. Blanche Caffiere, "Hints of Future Heights in Extraordinary Little Boy," *Christian Science Monitor,* July 20, 1995: 17.
3. Tom Peters, *The Pursuit of WOW! Every Person's Guide to Topsy-Turvy Times* (New York: Random House, 1994), 42.

10 USING TECHNOLOGY TO TELL YOUR LIBRARY'S STORY

Are the Internet and commercial online services like America Online viable tools for communicating your library's message? Consider the following:

- As of September 1994, an estimated 30 million people were connected to the Internet in 148 countries.
- Every 30 minutes, a new network joins the Internet.
- According to *Internet World* magazine, two new user accounts are added to the Internet every four minutes.
- According to *Boardwatch* magazine, most of the 60,000 bulletin board systems in the United States will be connected to the Internet by the end of 1995.
- Online computers services such as Prodigy, Compuserve, and America Online, have a combined subscriber base of more than six million people.
- Bulletin board systems host more than 20 million regular posters in the United States alone.
- The World Wide Web is growing by 20 percent per month.[1]

Based on these statistics, the chances are good that some members of the audience in your community are Internet users. In addition, the rapid growth of the Internet and other online services indicates that it won't be long before you will be able to reach even more of your audience electronically. While Internet access also increases the information resources that you can make available to your library's patrons, the Internet offers exciting possibilities for new public relations activities. Now is the time to start thinking of the Internet as a communications tool; when it becomes the obvious choice for telling your library's story and promoting your programs and events, you will have experience and success in using it and your patrons will be accustomed to receiving electronic communications from you.

You must consider, just as for other communications tools, whether or not electronic communications techniques are appropriate for your message and audience. Is it logical that your audience will have access to e-mail and/or the World Wide Web? In a college or university where every student has an e-mail address, it makes sense for the library to use electronic communications techniques. On the other hand, you may find that not many senior citizens or single parents in your community have computers with an Internet connection. Statistics may be available in your community describing the demographic breakdown of households that have Internet access. Obtaining this information will be important as you consider whether or not to use electronic communications tools.

Access is always an important issue for libraries, and many librarians are concerned that technology will widen the gap between the information "haves" and "have-nots." In his book *Being Digital*, Nicholas Negroponte makes an interesting point about who does and doesn't have access. He says,

> Some people worry about the social divide between the information-rich and the information-poor, the haves and the have-nots, the First and Third Worlds. But the real cultural divide is going to be generational. When I meet an adult who tells me he has discovered CD-ROM, I can guess that he has a child between five and ten years old. When I meet someone who tells me she has discovered America Online, there is probably a teenager in their house. . . . Both are being taken for granted by children the same way adults don't think about air (until it is missing).[2]
>
> Based on Negroponte's opinion, you may have a better chance of reaching younger audiences with your electronic communication. Young adults may be a great place to start.

This chapter explores Internet functions, such as e-mail and the World Wide Web, and how your library might consider using them to promote its programs, services, and resources. It does not provide technical information about how to set up or manage those activities. There are many other resources and Internet consultants available who can help you learn how to do that. As you think about the possibility of using e-mail or a home page on the World Wide Web as a communications tool for your library, you will probably want to think about "parallel publishing" the same information elsewhere. In light of access issues, this seems to be the best overall strategy when using electronic communications tools—at least for the moment.

THE INTERNET AS A PUBLIC RELATIONS TOOL

If your library has access to the Internet, either through a direct connection or an Internet provider, you may also have the ability to participate in a variety of Internet activities. You may be able send e-mail, participate in or host a listserv, access or develop a home page on the World Wide Web, and post to or develop and manage a news group. All of these activities have potential as tools for telling your library's story.

E-MAIL

You can use electronic mail to send personal notes and to transport documents or other files. One of the nicest things about electronic mail is that it arrives quickly and yet it doesn't interrupt the recipient like a phone call. You may want to consider using e-mail to communicate with local members of the media. You can send a news release to a specific reporter with a personal note, a thank-you note for a reporter's coverage of a story, or information about a new book that the reporter might be interested in. E-mail simplifies maintaining a relationship with the media.

Your library may also want to set up a general e-mail address for patrons to send questions about your programs and services. Such an arrangement prevents a lot of e-mail from going to anyone's individual mailbox and you give users a simple way to contact the library electronically even if they don't know who can answer their question. If you do this, however, monitoring incoming mail and either answering it or forwarding it to the appropriate person must be done on a regular and consistent basis, possibly twice per day. And it is important that responses are sent from "real people" rather than this general library mailbox. Attaching a person's name or signature to the response adds to the credibility and accountability of the information and it makes what could be a somewhat impersonal electronic encounter more personal.

LISTSERVS

Another way to use e-mail to promote your library is to participate in listservs. Listservs are electronic discussion groups. There are thousands of listservs including many focusing on areas of interest to librarians. After you join a listserv, you can send an e-mail message to the listserv. Once you have "posted" a message, everyone who subscribes to the listserv receives that message by e-mail. Some mailing lists are unmoderated; all mail sent to them is automatically forwarded to all list members. Other lists are moderated; someone actually reads all the messages sent to the list and makes decisions about whether to edit or post them. Still other lists are simply for the distribution of information and subscribers are not able to post to them at all.

If you decide to try using listservs to promote your library in your community, you should first find out how many local lists there are. This may not be easy. There are already 10,000 or more lists on the Internet. Talk to other individuals involved in communications in your community. If your city is involved in Internet communication, check with the technology office and find out what information they have. If you are in a school, inquire about what lists your school district has already set up and whether or not you are eligible to subscribe to them. If you are at a college or university, find out if student or faculty lists are already set up that you could use on a regular basis to disseminate information about your library.

Once you discover the lists that your target audiences might be subscribing to, subscribe yourself and "lurk" for a few weeks. You might also send an e-mail to the list manager and find out what the rules of conduct—"netiquette"—are for that list. Some lists, for example, don't want subscribers post promoting goods or services that they are selling. Tell the list manager that you are from the library and would occasionally like to post messages that might be helpful to the list's subscribers and that would probably also promote your library. In most cases, you will probably be told that you are welcome to participate in the list in this way.

Once you have something to share and understand the tone of the list, post! For example, if you are participating in a list for students at your university and students are complaining about not having good locations for their study groups, you might want to post a message about the study rooms at your library that they can schedule for their groups. Or if you are participating in a list for senior citizens in your community and they start to discuss the lack of local services for seniors, post information about the books-by-mail and senior programming services that your library provides.

When posting to a listserv, remember that the Internet is often more informal than other communications tools. Your messages will be more effective if they sound as if they came from a person and not as if you are just regurgitating policy or reprinting news releases.

You may want to start one or several lists of your own. All you need to do this is an e-mail address and access to a list manager program. Check with your Internet service provider for help in establishing a list. You could start a list designed specifically for teenagers to talk about books, the list could be managed collaboratively by the school and public libraries in your community, to promote new library materials or share information about programming for teens.

You could actually set up several book discussion lists and ask library staff members to moderate them. List participants never have to leave their homes and the librarian moderators can do the work when they have time available rather than at a regularly scheduled time.

Another idea is just to set up a library information list. This list might be one where subscribers only receive information and are not able to post. You can use such a list to disseminate all types of information about your library, such as a list of new books, holiday closure schedules, or highlights from a library board meeting. This type of list could help your patrons feel as if they are part of your library's community.

If you decide to develop and manage any type of listserv, it will be important, particularly in the beginning, to be sure that there is consistent activity on it. For the first few weeks, you might want to post something every day or every other day. If you set up a general information list, you might want to continue posting a daily message for the life of the list. You will need to prepare a description of each list explaining its topic, whether or not it is moderated, who is eligible to participate, and how to subscribe and unsubscribe. This description will be sent to each subscriber and can be used when you promote your lists.

NEWSGROUPS

A newsgroup is another way to share information on a topic in which you are interested. The difference between a listserv and a newsgroup is that one is passive and the other is active. When you send a message to a listserv, all members of the list receive it whether they want to or not. When you send a message to a newsgroup, the message is posted on an electronic bulletin board; anyone can read that message at any time. The message does not appear in an individual's mailbox. Like listservs, newsgroups can be either moderated or unmoderated. In order to access newsgroups, your Internet connection must include a newsreader.

If you think posting to newsgroups might help share your library's story, find out about local newsgroups just as you would listservs. Once you discover the groups available, you can start to read them (including several months of old posts to get a sense of the tenor and topics discussed), and then wait for your opportunity to post. It is always important to lurk for awhile before posting to determine what is appropriate for the discussion.

Starting a newsgroup of your own is different from starting a listserv. A newsgroup resides in the storage space of any Internet service provider who subscribes to it. So, if service providers don't subscribe to your newsgroup, you won't have much activity. Your newsgroup will exist, however, within a hierarchy of other newsgroups, such as miscellaneous (misc) or recreational (rec). If your newsgroup is a part of a hierarchy that the service provider subscribes to, then its users will have access to it.

To start a newsgroup, propose your group name and topic on news.announce.newsgroups and request a discussion about it. During the discussion, describe your specific plans for the group, such as topics to be discussed and whether or not it will be moderated. After 30 days of discussion, members of newsgroups decide whether or not the new newsgroup is appropriate. If response is favorable, you develop an official name and then call for an official vote among the newsgroup members. The voting period lasts 21 days. If the vote is affirmative, your group is automatically subscribed to by most service providers.

WORLD WIDE WEB

The World Wide Web is a system designed to help users navigate from site to site on the Internet. The Web uses "hyperlinks" that allow you to select a highlighted word to connect to another document linked with that word. A home page is the page you see when you connect to a Web site. It is created using hypertext markup language (html) and usually includes color, graphics, text, and links to other Web pages. To have a Web site, your library must either have a Web server, an Internet service provider, or another organization that will provide space for your Web site on its server.

At the moment, Web sites are all the rage. Companies, organizations, and even individuals are mounting their own pages on a daily basis. Everybody, including libraries, wants to have a Web presence. Your library may want to develop its own Web page or it may become a part of the city, school district, or university's Web site.

Libraries use Web pages to link to information resources on the World Wide Web. A Web site can become another way for a library to extend its access to information not owned by the library. Sites are also wonderful ways to promote your library's programs and services. For example, The Foley Center Library at Gonzaga University in Spokane, Washington, uses its Web page to provide information on the history and collections of the library, access to its online public catalog, and information about its Friends group. Houston Public Library provides all types of user information on its Web page, including how to get a library card, a calendar of events, and information about the library's special programs and collections. Other libraries have an electronic copy of their newsletter accessible via their Web page.

If you have Internet access, search for library Web sites. Web "surfing" will provide you with lots of creative ideas for things you might want to include on your library's home page. A Web presence is a great way for your library to promote itself both locally and nationally and to demonstrate that your staff and services are on the cutting edge of technology.

To develop a Web page, you have several options. You can download development software from the Internet. This is usually shareware and there is a small fee for using it. It comes with instructions and is easy to use. In addition, many online services, such as America Online and MSN (Microsoft Network), offer software and Web space for their subscribers.

Another option is to hire a Web architect. Like graphic designers, designers of Web pages come in a variety of skills and pricing levels. One current trend is for young high school entrepreneurs to market their services as Web page designers. It is important, however, to be sure that whoever you hire to design your library's Web page has some knowledge of graphic design as well as the language for the development of the page. If you invest money in your library's graphic identify, you want it to be reflected in your electronic promotional materials as well as in your print materials. Many graphic designers are becoming Web architects as well as developers of print materials. The same firm that developed your print graphic identity may be able to work with you on your Web presence and provide you with the tools for maintaining the site yourself.

For a complete discussion of developing Web pages for libraries, see *Using the World Wide Web and Creating Home Pages: A How-to-Do-It Manual for Librarians* by Ray E. Metz and Gail Junion-Metz (Neal-Schuman, 1996).

CREATING YOUR OWN BULLETIN BOARD SERVICE (BBS)

A bulletin board service (BBS) is an electronic version of the old corkboard. All you need to set one up is a computer, server, BBS software, a modem, and phone lines. Bulletin board services typically have three major sections—messages, files, and conference rooms. The messages are the corkboard section where anyone can post, the files area contains documents that people can read but not necessarily respond to, and the conference rooms provide people with the opportunity to participate in real-time discussions on particular topics.

If your library decides that a bulletin board service is the appropriate communications tool for your message and audience, the message area can function as a newsgroup. You can designate message areas for topics, such as discussions of small business resources, good books for children, or genealogy research. The file area might be where you post your calendar of events, library policies, board minutes, lists of recent acquisitions, or news releases. The conference rooms can be your chance to host electronic programming. You can ask a local expert on gardening to host a discussion every Wednesday from 2 to 4 p.m. and then promote that program. A library staff person who also participates in the discussion can promote library resources as the expert provides gardening information and tips. Or you can use the conference rooms to hold periodic focus groups on library programs and services. A bulletin board service allows you to reach and serve patrons who might never visit your library.

In addition, reporters and editors who access your bulletin board service can retrieve your news releases, read the full text of your board minutes, and access other policy documents and materials that you have in your files. "The job of the PR person is to make the reporter's job easier, and the BBS does that."[3]

MAINTENANCE

When deciding if you have the resources available for electronic public relations, remember to budget time for updating and maintaining your vehicles, particularly Web sites and bulletin board services. Links from your Web site to other Web pages should be checked regularly for accuracy. If users visit your site and consistently find out-of-date information, they will stop viewing it as a valuable resource. A staff person must be assigned the responsibility for and be vigilant about updating the information on a regular basis.

ONLINE EXPRESSION

Before you begin using electronic tools to communicate your library's message, familiarize yourself with the symbols and language of the Internet. For example, "emoticons" are a simple way to communicate emotions without using words. You can

> smile: :-)
> frown: :-(
> wink: ;-)

Acronyms are also used in communication on the Internet. For example:

> IMHO: in my humble opinion
> BTW: by the way
> LOL: laughing out loud
> ROTFL: rolling on the floor laughing
> FAQ: frequently asked question

There are books available that provide you with many more examples of this Internet shorthand. Familiarizing yourself with it will save you key strokes and make you look Internet-savvy when you start posting.

Also, remember that every post you make represents your library. Be as careful about grammar and spelling as you would in any printed communication.

SPREAD THE WORD

If you decide to use the Internet to share your library's story, remember to publicize what you are doing. Spread the word about your bulletin board service, add your library's e-mail and Web page addresses to your letterhead. Send a letter to the press telling them about the kinds of documents they can access via the files on your bulletin board. Developing and maintaining electronic communications vehicles is time-consuming. You will want to make the most of their availability—particularly if you are trying to position your library as technologically up-to-date.

NOTES

1. Jay Conrad Levinson, and Charles Rubin. *Guerrilla Marketing Online: The Entrepreneur's Guide to Earning Profits on the Internet* (New York: Houghton Mifflin, 1995), 5.
2. Nicholas Negroponte. *Being Digital* (New York: Random House, 1995), p. 6.
3. Lawrence Ragan Communications, Inc., "Use Electronic Bulletin Boards to Improve Every Aspect of Your Communication Function." *Technology for Communicators: Ideas for Communicating in a Wired World*, (Chicago: Lawrence Ragan Communications, n.d.): 2.

11 PROGRAMS AND SPECIAL EVENTS AS COMMUNICATIONS TOOLS

Programs and special events provide you with opportunities to tell your library's story, to attract new audiences to your library, to make new connections in the community, and to have a lot of fun! You can use programs and special events to tell your library's story—both directly and indirectly. Sometimes the program or special event will blatantly communicate the message; at other times it will communicate it subliminally. For example, if your library's message is to encourage use of its local history collection, a series of adult programs on topics related to the resources in the collection directly communicates your public relations message. On the other hand, if you want to communicate that your library is a community center, you may want to encourage a variety of community groups to sponsor programs in your meeting room. While the topics of these programs may or may not be related to materials in your library's collection, such programming quietly communicates your "library as community center" message.

One advantage of carefully planned programs and special events is that they bring people into your library. For example, a series of evening workshops appealing to parents of preschoolers, with an accompanying storytime, can be an effective strategy for helping parents develop the "library habit" and will, ultimately, increase your library's circulation and gate count. Or, if you want parents to see the resources and excitement of your school library media center, hosting a special evening reception during National Library Week that showcases student work may be one strategy for communicating your message.

WHAT ARE PROGRAMS?

Library programs disseminate information to participants. They are public relations tools, but they are also part of any library's services to the community. Therefore, it is important that library programming not be planned in isolation by the individual or team responsible for public relations. Library staff in service areas should be involved in the program planning process. In fact, they may bring program ideas to the public relations team and ask for help in developing and promoting them. For example, the business reference librarian at your library may want to do a series of programs on the services and resources that your library can provide to small businesses. She might be willing to design the content for the programs, but be stuck when it comes to targeting audiences or developing promotional materials. This is an excellent opportunity for staff collaboration.

TYPES OF PROGRAMS

The types of programs that libraries can present go far beyond the traditional storyhours and book discussion groups. Libraries host informational presentations on a myriad of topics, sponsor film festivals and special showings of movies, provide free concert opportunities—the possibilities are endless. And, library programs can be geared for a wide variety of audiences, too—children, young adults, parents, senior citizens, small business owners, corporate executives, homemakers, college students; again, the possibilities are endless.

When planning successful library programs, the key is to think creatively and try not to duplicate the effort of other community organizations. For example, if your library would like to offer a program on how to build bluebird houses and attract bluebirds, do some research to find out if anyone else in the community is offering a similar program. You may discover that the Audubon Society has offered that program twice in the past; planning and hosting your own program on that topic would duplicate their efforts. You may also discover that the Audubon Society is looking for a location for this year's program and you might offer them your library's meeting room for their presentation. In addition, if you offer to help promote the program, they might be willing to list your library as a cosponsor for the program. This turns out to be a positive solution for everyone—you don't spend time developing a program that already exists and the Audubon Society gets a free location and increased promotion for a program they were considering doing anyway.

At other times, you may discover, for example, that a program is already being sponsored by another organization and that they already have a location. This is your opportunity to offer to develop a resource list for distribution at the program. Such a list promotes your library and its resources on the program topic. Again, you aren't duplicating the other organization's effort, but you are supporting it.

Of course, there will be times when you have a unique program idea that should be developed by your library. This is the time when you should rely on your library staff's expertise and community connections and on your communications plan and relationship with the local media.

PROGRAM DEVELOPMENT AND PLANNING

To communicate any message for your library effectively, programs must be carefully planned and effectively promoted. It is futile to plan an informative adult or children's program if you don't put equal effort into recruiting an audience for it. On the other hand, you don't want to promote a program until you are sure that you can give participants what your promotional materials promise. Time is precious and when you ask people to attend a program, you are asking them to give up some of their time. If participants don't feel the program they attended was worth their time, you may create a negative public perception of your library. In addition, if community volunteers develop a wonderful program, but no one shows up because you failed to promote the program, you have damaged their perception of your library also. You must commit time and energy to both content planning and promotion for a program. If you cannot, you should consider using a different communications tool.

On the other hand, just like any aspect of public relations/communications, program planning and promotion is not an exact science. You can plan the best program in the world, and promote it in a targeted and informative way, but if there is a blizzard on the night of the program, the success of the program in terms of attendance is really out of your control. There are things that you can do, however, when planning your program to help ensure your success.

Before you decide to do a program, make sure it has a specific purpose and relationship to your public relations goal. Programming for the sake of programming (or a special event planned with no clear goal) has the potential to send you along a damaging detour on the road to your public relations goal.

Need, audience, format, and necessary resources are the first things that you should think about when planning any library program. Each time you consider holding a program you may want to complete a program development form similar to the example in Figure 11.1.

FIGURE 11.1 Program/Special Event Development Form

Program/special event name:

Program/special event content or activity:

Public relations goal or objective related to this program/special event:

Need: Why should we plan this program/special event?

Audience: Who are we targeting with this program/special event? What age range?

Format: What format should the program/special event take? Should it be held in the morning, afternoon, or evening? Should it be lecture-only or interactive? Will there be a movie or other performance?

Resources: What resources are required to present this program/special event? Does the presenter or performer require a fee? Approximately how much staff time will be consumed by planning, promoting, and hosting the program/special event? Will there be equipment to be rented? Will we need to rent a space to hold the program/special event in?

After completing the form, think carefully about the program you are considering. Will you get enough bang for your buck? Is the potential audience large enough to justify the staff time and other resources that the program will need? Does the program help you achieve your public relations goal? This is basically a judgment call. If you or your programming planning committee answers "yes" to these questions, then planning must begin in earnest.

Plenty of lead time for planning and promotion will be key to the success of your program. At least three months is usually best. Sometimes, however, you may get an opportunity to present a program that is too good to ignore even though you won't have sufficient planning time. Maybe a best-selling author is visiting your town and is willing to make a presentation, or a popular jazz group wants to donate a performance. You may decide the opportunity is worth working overtime to pull off the program. In general, however, you will want to work with 12 weeks of lead time.

Planning a program requires certain basic steps. If you follow these steps with sufficient lead time, you have a good chance of success. A basic program /special event planning checklist, based on 12 weeks of lead time, appears in Figure 11.2.

PROGRAM EVALUATION

Evaluation of your programs will provide you with an important tool for future program planning. Using a simple evaluation form, you can learn what participants thought about your program and what other types of programs they would like your library to offer. Keeping your evaluation form short and easy to complete will increase the number of participants who fill it out. Think carefully about what you want to learn and then design your evaluation form to get that information. See Figure 11.3 for a sample program evaluation form.

If you ask your participants to take the time to complete this evaluation, you should take their input seriously. Compiling the results and relying on them to plan your library's future programming will be important to your success. Your result will be library programs that have developed from community interest and need. Through continual evaluation you will learn what you are doing right and what you need to improve in future programs.

FIGURE 11.2 Program/Special Event Planning Checklist

12 weeks before program/special event

Complete Program/Special Event Development Form.

Determine date, time, and location for program/special event. Check that there aren't any competing activities planned for the same date.

Secure any necessary funding for the program/special event.

Develop promotional plan for program/special event.

8 weeks before program/special event

Confirm in writing presenters and other involved participants.

Decide if the program/special event has any direct links to materials in your library's collection and whether or not you will prepare a book list or display for the function.

Develop evaluation form.

1 week before program/special event

Contact presenter to confirm audiovisual and other needs.

Make name badges for presenters and other special guests.

3 hours before program/special event

Check space to be sure that audiovisual equipment is set up and working, and that room is set up correctly.

1 hour before program/special event

Be available to greet presenters and participants.

Day after the program/special event

Write thank-you notes to everyone who helped make the program/special event possible.

Compile results of evaluation and analyze the implications for the future.

FIGURE 11.3 Program Evaluation

Please circle the number that most closely describes your evaluation of this program.

This program was informative.

Very		Moderately		Not at all
5	4	3	2	1

This program was entertaining.

Very		Moderately		Not at all
5	4	3	2	1

I would recommend this program to my friends.

Very		Moderately		Not at all
5	4	3	2	1

The location for this program was convenient.

Very		Moderately		Not at all
5	4	3	2	1

The time for this program was convenient.

Very		Moderately		Not at all
5	4	3	2	1

Overall, I rate the program as

Excellent		Average		Poor
5	4	3	2	1

FIGURE 11.3 (cont.)

Other programs that I would like to attend (please list):

_____

_____

_____

_____

Other comments:

_____

_____

_____

_____

Please add my name and address to your mailing list for future programs:

Name _____

Address _____

City, State, Zip Code _____

Thank you for attending Anytown Public Library's program!

WHAT ARE SPECIAL EVENTS?

Special events may or may not be an opportunity to share information with participants. They may or may not raise funds for your library. All special events, however, are "special"—they are unique or different activities from what your library offers on a regular basis. A special event occurs once and has a particular purpose. Example of special events include groundbreaking or ribbon-cutting ceremonies for a new library building, a reception or banquet, or a special fundraising event, such as a theater benefit or fun run.

If planned carefully and used sparingly, special events can put the community spotlight on your library and can reward library users, attract new users, and, in some cases, raise funds for your library. However, if the event is a disappointment for attendees, or if it seems as if your library is hosting a special event every week, the impact of this communications tool will be diminished. You rarely have a second chance with a special event.

Before you begin to plan a special event, ask yourself if it is truly worthy of your time and energy and the focus of the community. Think about how long it has been since your library sponsored a similar event. What was the community reaction? What should you do differently this time? For example, cutting the ribbon on your new library building definitely merits a celebration, media coverage, and lots of hoopla. In contrast, the addition of 250 new titles to your video collection might be celebrated in a different, more low-key manner, such as a newsletter article or a special in-library display. Don't "cry wolf" with your special events. When your library says it has something to celebrate or focus on, make sure it is worthy. Planning special events takes lots of time and hard work, too; be sure that the purpose of the event merits the effort.

SPECIAL EVENT DEVELOPMENT AND PLANNING

The same steps to plan a program for your library should be used to plan a special event. The key is to give yourself plenty of lead time and to be sure that there is a relationship between your event and your public relations/communications goal.

No detail is too small to write down and assign someone to be responsible for. Careful attention to detail will help make your event special. It will be obvious to participants that nothing was overlooked and that this event is very important to your library and your community.

SPECIAL EVENT SPONSORSHIPS

Special events offer local businesses and corporations the opportunity for relationship building through sponsorships. By providing support for your event, either in terms of fiscal or human resources, a business or corporation can, by association, cash in on your library's goodwill and good reputation—and you get to put on your event. If you work with a sponsor, you can develop a mutually beneficial relationship.

Reading, libraries, and books are all important values in our society, and most corporate sponsors would want to be associated with events related to them. Pizza Hut and Jell-O have sponsored major national reading promotion programs. In 1985–1986, more than seven million children participated in Pizza Hut's Book-It program. The company invested $50 million worth of free pizza in the program. The average number of books read by each student increased over the previous year by 300 percent, reading levels improved by 53 percent and reading enjoyment increased by 78 percent. This was a win-win situation for Pizza Hut and for reading and libraries.[1]

Once you have decided that you want to have a special event, you may want to approach a local business or corporation for sponsorship. Think carefully about who might be most interested in your event. For example, the local electric power utility might have expressed a strong interest in children and education and you are planning a huge end-of-summer reading rally. Sounds like a perfect match! Develop the plan for your event, put a price tag on it, and make an appointment to see the appropriate person at the company. Better yet, do you know someone who has a connection with the company? Is one of your board members on the company's board? Explore all of these connections before going blithely off to pitch your event.

Also, think carefully about whether or not the company that you are approaching can actually afford your event. Design your proposal in such a way to indicate that you are offering them the opportunity for sole sponsorship, but that, if necessary, you will work with multiple sponsors. Develop your list of sponsor benefits, however, it is more beneficial to be a sole sponsor than one of several. Develop and pitch a realistic budget. Above all, don't undersell the value of being associated with your library and your event. Some events-marketing consultants recommend putting a price tag on being associated with your library's name. Your level of involvement with corporate sponsors and the actual promotional market may not be big enough or sophisticated enough to merit this type of sponsorship fee, however. A proposal outline for a special event sponsorship appears in Figure 11.4

Make sure that the recognition that you provide sponsors is commensurate with their contribution. If a sponsor gives you $500, for example, to fund an event that costs a total of $5,000, putting its name on a billboard is probably excessive. In addition, if you begin offering a lot of corporate-sponsored events, you may want to develop a plan of levels of sponsorship. Such a plan ensures equity in your recognition program. Sponsorship levels are usually based on dollar amounts. A simple example appears in Figure 11.5.

FIGURE 11.4 Special Event Sponsorship Proposal Outline

Name of special event:

Purpose:

Date, time, location:

Description of event: Include names of participants, types of activities that will be included, etc. For example, if you are planning a fun run, discuss who your target audience will be. If you are planning an open house, describe the activities that will be happening in the library during the open house, who the celebrity guests might be, and who will be providing the entertainment.

Promotional plan for event: Develop your promotional plan before approaching the sponsor. This will help the sponsor to see the opportunities for recognition of their sponsorship.

Sponsor recognition opportunities: Detail the times and places where the sponsor will be recognized. Examples include listing the sponsor's name on all special event promotional materials and/or introducing the sponsor's representatives during the event. Be very specific about the types of recognition you are prepared to provide.

Budget: Include the total budget for the event—not just the amount that you are asking the sponsor to fund. Include the time and materials that your library is providing for the event as "in-kind." This shows the sponsor that the event is important enough for the library to dedicate resources to it.

FIGURE 11.5 Sample Sponsorship Recognition Program

MIDDLEFIELD PUBLIC LIBRARY
SPONSORSHIP RECOGNITION PROGRAM

Gold Sponsor ($10,000–$25,000)

- Name on plaque in Main Library lobby
- Special sticker for corporate officers' library cards recognizing their support of the library
- Name of corporation included on all program or event promotional materials
- Announcement of sponsorship at program or event
- Listed as Gold Sponsor once per year in monthly newsletter

Silver Sponsor ($5,000–$9,999)

- Special sticker for corporate officers' library cards recognizing their support of the library
- Name of corporation included on all program or event promotional materials
- Announcement of sponsorship at program or event
- Listed as Silver Sponsor once per year in monthly newsletter

Bronze Sponsor ($2,000–$4,999)

- Name of corporation included on all program or event promotional materials
- Announcement of sponsorship at program or event
- Listed as Bronze Sponsor once per year in monthly newsletter

Platinum Sponsor ($500–$1,999)

- Announcement of sponsorship at program or event
- Listed as Platinum Sponsor once per year in monthly newsletter

Sponsor ($100–$499)

- Listed as Sponsor once per year in monthly newsletter

SPECIAL EVENT EVALUATION

While it is important to evaluate your library's special events, the activities involved may not be conducive to the completion of a formal evaluation form. It is hard to ask participants at an open house or a fun run to fill out a form. In fact, it may detract from the festive atmosphere and your completion rate may suffer. The easiest way to evaluate a special event may be to set some goals and then evaluate the success of the event in relationship to these goals.

For example, if your school library is having an open house, you could set the following goals:

- To have the event attended by a minimum of 125 parents.
- To have the event covered by at least one television station and the community newspaper.

Then you can measure your success against these goals. Asking attendees to sign a guest book is a nice way to measure your attendance and you can monitor media coverage of the event. In addition, you may want to add some qualitative information to your evaluation of the event. When you meet to discuss what worked about your event and what didn't, you will want to ask school faculty members and students to share their impressions of the event and the impressions that participants shared with them. This information will help you with future planning and help you evaluate the success of your event.

PROMOTING PROGRAMS AND SPECIAL EVENTS

You promote programs and special events to get people to act. You want them to participate in your program or to attend your special event. In most cases, you aren't simply trying to create a positive perception of your program or event. Therefore, you will want to develop a promotional plan that will encourage people to take some type of action.

CHOOSING YOUR PROGRAM/SPECIAL EVENT PROMOTIONAL TOOL

All of the communications tools described in this book are possibilities for promoting your library's program or event. You will have to decide which ones you are going to use based on the audience you want to reach, the lead time you have before the program or event, and the budget that is available to you.

The key to encouraging people to attend your program or special event is to be sure that whatever communications tool you select includes all of the information that a person needs in order to attend your program or event. Use the checklist in Figure 11.6 to review your promotional materials.

Each time you develop a flyer or brochure for a program or event, review it against this information checklist or an expanded one that you may develop. It may seem obvious that you would include all of this information, but even the most experienced event planner or public relations person can tell you about a time when critical information was omitted from promotional material—and the unfortunate result.

Another important factor in promoting your library's program or special event will be to think carefully about where the promotional materials should be distributed. Flyers promoting summer reading are a natural for distribution through the public schools. If your university library is hosting an open house, flyers should be stuffed in student mailboxes or a broadcast message sent to their e-mail accounts. You probably won't reach the audience you want if you just make the promotional materials available in your library—particularly if one of your goals to encourage library use by nonusers.

FIGURE 11.6 Program/Special Event Promotional Materials Information Checklist

- Clear description of the program or event
- Date and time
- Location
- Cost (if any)
- Whether or not registration is required and, if so, how to register
- Age that the program or event is geared to (especially important for children's programs)
- Where to call for more information
- Event sponsors

EXHIBITS AND DISPLAYS

Like programs and special events, library exhibits and displays are both an information service and a public relations activity. They can help to increase your library's visibility and promote its services and collections. In addition, by allowing schools and other community groups to exhibit in your library, you can increase library use and bring in new audiences. Most parents will want to visit the library to see their child's artwork displayed there, even if they don't normally use the library. While they are there, they may see the available resources and services and change their perception of your library. In some cases, they may even become library users.

Before you begin to plan an exhibits program for your library, decide whether or not you have the space available. You need room for both the exhibit and for participants to view it. The exhibits that you book for your library may come with display boards or you may have to look into building or purchasing some for your own use.

You must decide the goal of your exhibits program. Where does it fit in terms of your overall public relations/communications plan? What goals and objectives does it help you fulfill? Again, like all other communications tools, an exhibits program needs to have a purpose and a plan.

If you decide that an exhibits program will help you achieve your public relations/communications goals, the next step is to develop an exhibits policy. The principles in the American Library Association's *Exhibit Spaces and Bulletin Boards: An Interpretation of the Library Bill of Rights* will help you develop this policy. The policy should include your procedure and criteria for accepting exhibits, the length of time that exhibits will be on display, and the security and insurance that your library will or will not provide for exhibits.

Finally, you need to develop an application for exhibit space. The application will help you select exhibits for display and can also be used when you are promoting the fact that your library has exhibit space available. A sample application for exhibit space appears in Figure 11.7.

EVALUATING YOUR EXHIBITS PROGRAM

You will want to evaluate the success of your exhibits program on an annual basis. One way to get continual qualitative feedback on your exhibits is to provide a guest book for visitors to

FIGURE 11.7 Application for Exhibit Space

Name _____

Organization (if any) _____

Address _____

Phone _____ Fax _____ E-mail_____

Preferred dates for exhibit _____

Title of exhibit_____

Number of pieces in exhibit _____

Average size of pieces _____

Have you exhibited at Middlefield Public Library in the past? _____

If yes, what dates? _____

I have read and will abide by Middlefield Public Library's exhibits policy. I understand that Middlefield Public Library does not provide any insurance or security for its exhibits. My artwork will be displayed at my own risk.

Signature _____ Date _____

Return to: Middlefield Public Library Exhibits
            123 Main Street
            Middlefield, Ohio 44444

DO NOT WRITE BELOW THIS LINE
_____

Application status:

_____Accepted   _____Denied

Date booked _____

Date letter mailed to applicant _____

sign and write comments in. This information will help you to plan future exhibits and to decide which exhibits were particularly successful and should be booked again. In addition, you may wish to send your exhibitors an evaluation form after hosting their exhibit. This is an opportunity to receive feedback from their perspective and again will help with future planning.

Another way to evaluate the success of an exhibit is to compare your library's gate count during the exhibit to the gate count for the same dates in the previous year. If there is a significant increase, this increase might be linked to the popularity of your exhibit.

CONCLUSION

Programs, special events, and exhibits can be both fun and informative! If carefully planned and promoted, they can provide an important information resource for your community as well as further your public relations goals. They bring people into your library who might not normally visit, giving them a chance to see the services and materials that your library provides. Best of all, programs, special events, and exhibits have the potential to enhance the public's perception of your library and to create new library users.

NOTES

1. Thomas L. Harris, *The Marketer's Guide to Public Relations: How Today's Top Companies Are Using the New PR to Gain a Competitive Edge.* (New York: John Wiley & Sons, 1991.), 234.

12 CREATING A PROFESSIONAL NETWORK

In the beginning, books such as this one and workshops and seminars will help guide you in your public relations efforts. You will get your ongoing inspiration, support, and new ideas, however, from the relationships you create within a network of peers who are doing communications work both in libraries and other organizations. Making connections with other individuals will give the chance to share experiences, discuss challenges, and develop creative new approaches to promoting your library and its programs, services, and resources. The opportunity for creating that network can be found in state library associations, through the American Library Association, and in public relations and communications professional associations.

STATE LIBRARY ASSOCIATIONS

Most state library associations have committees or sections whose specific focus is library public relations. The individuals involved in these groups include both librarians who do public relations work as an additional duty and full-time library public relations people. The activities of these groups range from planning conference programs and workshops to producing newsletters and tip sheets for their colleagues. In addition, many of these groups function as a support group for people who are doing the same work in different libraries. This support group provides you with an opportunity to discuss, with individuals other than those you deal with on a day-to-day basis, the challenges that you face in your library and community. Plus, it provides you with a chance to share your creative solutions to challenges that you have faced.

Contact the library association in your state for information about the type of public relations networking opportunities available. If there aren't any, you might wish to form a section or interest group with some of your colleagues who are doing similar work. Be proactive!

AMERICAN LIBRARY ASSOCIATION OPPORTUNITIES

The American Library Association (ALA) provides opportunities for networking with library public relations colleagues on a national basis. Two formal opportunities are the Public Relations Section of the Library Administration and Management Association and the Marketing Section of the Public Library Association. In addition, most of ALA's other divisions have public relations–focused committees and task forces. Involvement in these groups will provide you with another level of networking beyond your state organization and with the opportunity to learn about what is happening in library public relations throughout the nation.

The public relations–focused programming offered at ALA's annual conference will offer you learning opportunities. You will see exemplary programs, learn about ALA's support for your local public relations efforts, and have a chance to judge what you are doing against what is happening in other libraries. In some instances you will glean terrific new ideas, and in other cases you will learn that what you are doing is exceptional compared to what others are doing. Both are valuable reasons for being involved in ALA.

For more information about ALA, its conferences, and opportunities to explore library public relations, contact the association at (800) 545-2433 or access its World Wide Web page at http://www.ala.org.

PROFESSIONAL ASSOCIATIONS

There are many associations, on both a local and national level, for public relations and communications professionals that you may wish to become involved with. Their members, like those of library organizations, include both full-time public relations professionals and individuals who have public relations duties as part of another position. Involvement in these groups will help you see your communications efforts in a different way. You will have the chance to network with people working in public relations and communications, in areas ranging from nonprofits to corporations and government. In addition to learning more about effective ways to communicate your library's message, you may make valuable contacts for your library by being active in one of these groups.

Do some research to determine which groups exist in your community and how active they are. Two of the major national associations that have local chapters are described below.

International Association of Business Communications (IABC)
One Hallidie Plaza, Suite 600
San Francisco, CA 94012
(800) 776-4222
http://www.iabc.com
IABC offers the opportunity to network with other communicators. Services to members include workshops, a subscription to *Communication World*, and annual local and national awards.

Public Relations Society of America (PRSA)
33 Irving Place
New York, NY 10003
(212) 995-2230
http://www.prsa.org
PRSA focuses on professional development and has more than 100 U.S. chapters.

PROFESSIONAL DEVELOPMENT

Taking advantage of high-quality professional development opportunities is important in communications, as in any professional area. It is particularly important constantly to be learning more about communications and public relations because the available technology and communications techniques are changing so rapidly and are becoming increasingly sophisticated. This learning process is a two-way street; you will want to participate in professional development opportunities and provide such opportunities for others.

PARTICIPATING

Organizations such as the ones described above will provide a wide variety of professional development and training opportunities. Some will be "how-to-do-it" presentations and others will focus on the more theoretical and philosophical aspects of communications. You will want to take advantage of both. Understanding how and why people retain information and react to different communications techniques will be as important to your work as honing your skills for speech writing or developing effective print promotional publications. Develop a communications professional development plan for yourself that includes a mixture of both the practical and the theoretical. Then use the theory that you learn in the practical application of your work.

PROVIDING

Sharing your library public relations and communications experiences with your colleagues through conference programs and other professional development events will provide you with another learning opportunity. By sharing your "lessons learned," you can help others to develop effective communications programs for their libraries. At the same time, they can provide you with tips for avoiding problems that they have encountered. In addition, presenting at local, state, and national meetings is good public relations for your school, community, or university. Through your presentation, you can demonstrate the exciting things that are happening at your institution and you create a positive public perception of your library and community. Community leaders and people who hold the purse strings will be impressed when they learn that an activity at your library has been selected for presentation at a national, state, or local conference.

INFORMAL NETWORKING AND SHARING

Some of your most valuable networking opportunities will be informal. You may learn more from the person you meet on the shuttle bus at a conference than you do during a formal presentation. Talk to the people you meet, ask them about their work, listen, learn, and share. Not only will you get valuable information during the encounter, you may also develop a relationship with a peer whom you can later call for assistance or advice. Collect your colleagues' business cards and nurture those relationships. Ask them to send you samples of the materials they are producing and send them copies of yours. These relationships will be invaluable, particularly when you face such public relations challenges as censorship attempts or funding decreases. Your colleagues will be able to provide ideas and support, and, when needed, they can be understanding friends.

Keeping your eyes open for great communications techniques—in all walks of your life—will also provide you with great new ideas. When you walk down the street, look at the billboards you encounter. What kind of interesting techniques are they employing in their communications efforts? What is the new, compelling approach that television or radio commercials are using? Look at the travel brochures that you pick up at a hotel, the direct-mail pieces that you receive, and other people's news releases. You'll see things that don't work and you'll know to avoid them. You'll see things that do work and you may be able to integrate them into your future efforts.

Start a file of samples of print pieces that you find particularly appealing and a file of those that you think have problems. These will basically become your print materials "do's" and "don'ts" files. When you are ready to develop a new publication, flipping through these files will help spark ideas and remind you of things to avoid.

Along the same line, when you get a great idea from a television ad or another communications tool, jot a few notes on a piece of paper and stick it in an ideas file or start a folder for those ideas on your computer. You may not have an application for the idea the moment you see it, but down the road it may fit the bill for a promotion.

ENTERING CONTESTS AND WINNING AWARDS

Many public relations and communications awards opportunities are available and several at the national level are specifically for library public relations. Entering these contests can be a valuable experience. It will help you to see how your work stands up against the work of others nationally and the application process may help you evaluate your efforts. In addition, when you win an award it emphasizes the quality of your public relations communications efforts to the individuals who are funding it, such as your library board or your principal or university administrator. It also demonstrates to your community the quality of the work being done by the library.

LIBRARY PUBLIC RELATIONS AWARD OPPORTUNITIES

Several important library public relations award opportunities are described below. By applying for them, you will share your library's work with the national network of libraries and will be able to learn more about what other libraries are doing to communicate their message to their communities.

John Cotton Dana Public Relations Awards

These awards, sponsored by the H.W. Wilson Company and the ALA's Library Administration and Management Association, are the most prestigious library public relations awards. All types of libraries are eligible to apply for the award by submitting a scrapbook describing their public relations program. Developing a scrapbook based on the application guidelines is time-consuming, so it is best to begin several months before the early February deadline. Compiling a John Cotton Dana Award scrapbook will provide you with a complete record of your public relations program and an opportunity to evaluate your program even if you aren't an award winner. An award is given to the best overall public relations program and citations are given for specific public relations projects. The John Cotton Dana Awards are presented during an afternoon tea held at the American Library Association's annual conference. There is no cash award, but an elegant certificate is presented.

For more information or an application form, write to Library Public Relations Department, H.W. Wilson Company, 950 University Avenue, Bronx, NY 10452.

"L. PeRCy Award" Award

This award, sponsored by the Library Public Relations Council (LPRC), recognizes excellence in six categories: newsletter, annual report, service brochure, book/material lists, summer reading program, and logo. For entry forms, contact David Bryant, Belleville Public Library, 221 Washington Avenue, Belleville, NJ 07109.

"Share the Wealth" Contest

Also sponsored by LPRC, this award judges "PR Bests" which are assembled and distributed to council members. To enter, submit five copies of any public relations item, such as a bookmark, flyer, annual report, or brochure. If your item is selected for the packet, you will be asked to provide 300 copies of your item. For entry forms, contact Cindy Czesak, Clifton Public Library, 292 Fiaget Avenue, Clifton, NJ 07013.

ALA Swap and Shop

Share your public relations materials at the annual Swap and Shop, sponsored by the Public Relations Section of the Library Administration and Management Association at the ALA's annual conference. You must submit 250 copies of each item. Visit the event and take home examples of library public relations materials from throughout the country.

Submit your best materials for the Swap and Shop "Best of Show." Certificates are awarded in categories such as bookmarks, annual reports, service brochures, and summer reading materials. For more information about Swap and Shop and its Best of Show competition, contact ALA at 50 E. Huron Street, Chicago, IL 60611, (800) 545–2433.

ALA Library Card Sign-Up Contest

This annual competition, held in cooperation with World Book, awards $1,000, $500, and $250 prizes to libraries with the largest increase in library card registration. Contact ALA Public Information Office for more information, at ALA, 50 E. Huron Street, Chicago, IL 60611, (800) 545-2433.

OTHER AWARDS

Communications professional organizations, such as PRSA and IABC, also have local and national award opportunities for public relations and communications efforts. You can learn more about them by contacting the associations or accessing their home pages on the World Wide Web. In addition, you may want to explore other local public relations awards offered by your community's advertising council or other groups. By applying for these awards, you will have the opportunity to compare your communications efforts to nonlibrary programs; you may learn that what you are doing holds up pretty well even in comparison to well-funded corporate efforts. High-quality, effective communications efforts win awards more often than slick, high-budgeted programs that do not communicate well.

WINNING AN AWARD AS A PR OPPORTUNITY

When your school, public, or academic library wins any type of award, you are presented with a wonderful public relations opportunity. You can issue a news release, hold an awards ceremony, or publish an article in your newsletter. You will want to strategize carefully how promoting your award-winning status fits into your overall communications plan. However you proceed, this type of recognition builds community pride and is a terrific "pat on the back" for staff who have dedicated a great deal of time and energy to your communications efforts.

The Awards Trap

While there are many beneficial reasons for submitting materials and winning public relations awards, be careful of falling into the awards trap—developing materials with a specific award in mind. Remember that the compelling factors in the development of your public relations/communications efforts must be your goals and the message that you want to communicate, not the criteria for a particular award. Make "We don't do public relations to win awards, we do public relations that wins awards!" your motto. Then when you do something that is really effective and you are really proud of, submit it and win an award!

NETWORKING IS HARD WORK

Once you become involved in a professional association and begin to build a network of colleagues in the public relations/communications professions, it will take time and energy to maintain that network. Attending meetings, following up with colleagues, and keeping abreast of the organization's programs and activities will be time-consuming. Weigh the time you invest against the benefits you get in terms of new ideas, avoiding pitfalls, and personal and professional support. Chances are you will find that the returns are many times your investment.

13 PUBLIC RELATIONS CHALLENGES IN DIFFERENT TYPES OF LIBRARIES

Different types of libraries (such as public, school, academic, and special libraries) have a lot in common. They follow basically the same philosophies of service and adhere to guiding principles such as the *Library Bill of Rights*. The public relations/communications planning process described in Chapter 2 is applicable to any type of library, and the communications tools and strategies described in the succeeding chapters are available and appropriate in varying degrees for public, school, academic, and special libraries. However, each type of library serves a different audience, has a unique purpose, and, as a result, each faces some different communications challenges and opportunities. In this chapter, public relations/communications activities at public, school, academic, and special libraries are explored through "success stories." These stories may not all have fairy-tale endings, but all of the efforts result in some degree of success. They offer realistic insights into the challenges of public relations in each type of library and the fact that, at times, success can be dangerous.

PUBLIC LIBRARIES

SUCCESS STORY

Middlefield Public Library serves a city of 45,000 citizens from two branches and one kiosk in a shopping mall. Susan Miller is the reference librarian responsible for public relations at Middlefield Public Library. She has 14 hours per week to devote to her public relations activities. Susan carefully and thoughtfully assembled a public relations advisory committee for her library and they are in the midst of implementing the public relations/communications plan that was developed.

Susan finds it hard, however, to find the time to deal with the communications activities detailed in the plan. A city funding crunch, a flood at one of the system's branch libraries, and a censorship challenge have put the library in the media spotlight and have taken up the small portion of time that Susan has to devote to public relations. In addition, just as she was about to launch a major promotion of the library's summer reading program, a community group began to protest the fact that the library has R-rated videos in its collection. Instead of headlines touting the exciting new summer reading program, the paper carried stories proclaiming that the public library was a "dangerous place for children." In fact, two of the corporate sponsors for summer reading reneged on their agreements in light of the video controversy.

Susan has seen some success from her planned public relations efforts. A promotional effort to increase homebound service has increased that program's circulation by 15 percent and a special mailing to parents of preschoolers has increased storytime attendance by twice the goal of 20 percent. Also, the library's overall circulation has increased by more than 25 percent, which, ironically, the staff attributes to renewed interest as a result of the news coverage provoked by the video and budget controversies.

PUBLIC LIBRARY PR CHALLENGES

This story might seem a bit extreme, but it is indicative of the kind of communications challenges that public librarians, particularly those who are only part-time public relations people, face. Issues arise that weren't planned and there don't seem to be enough hours in the day to deal with all of them. Creative public relations librarians, like Susan, do learn to capitalize on such issues and still achieve their goals, even if the approach is a little different from what they had planned.

In addition, public libraries face different public relations challenges according to their size. Small libraries usually have very small staffs and have the most difficult time finding time to engage in public relations activities. But they are also usually in small enough communities that obtaining coverage in the local media is easier and promotion of library programs and other events can occur by word-of-mouth as well as through planned public relations activities.

The bureaucratic structures that are usually a part of a large public library system can often get in the way of effective public relations. By the time a staff person receives clearance to give an interview or participate in an event, the moment of opportunity may be gone. The best and most effective public relations often happens in medium-size libraries. They are big enough to have the staff to manage the activities and yet they are small enough that they aren't restricted by a large bureaucracy and lots of red tape.

Another major challenge for public libraries is focusing their message. Public libraries have traditionally wanted to be all things to all people; often, when developing a public relations/communications plan, staff want to promote all of the library's programs and services. It is important to think carefully about what services need promotion during a particular time frame and also which services can tolerate being promoted. For example, if you launch a huge promotion of your books-by-mail service, you first need to be sure that you have the budget available to cover the costs of increased use. Or if the space you have for preschool storytime is already filled each week with 3-year-olds, your public relations efforts would probably be better focused on a different program or service. (It is not that preschool storytime isn't a valuable program that deserves promotion, but at the moment you don't have a lot of room for growth.)

Targeting a specific audience is another challenge for public libraries since they serve all members of a community. Again, careful thought is necessary to determine what group the library really wants to encourage to use its services. Public libraries not only serve all members of the community, but they can, at times, become a target for various community groups. Censors attack the library's collection; the genealogy club thinks that its collection should take over the entire first floor; a group of concerned citizens is upset that the library is throwing away withdrawn items. Because it is the "public" library, the public feels it has the right to voice its concerns over every practice in the library—and they do! The positive aspect is that members of the community who are aware of what is happening at their library and expressing their concerns are taking a great deal of ownership in this community-based institution. Creative public relations can take advantage of this ownership, particularly in times of crisis.

Finally, budget for public relations activities is always a challenge for public libraries. Community members, library board members, and others often have a difficult time understanding why a library needs a public relations program; they are hesitant to allow money from another area, like the materials budget, to fund it. The best strategy for changing mindsets in this area is to develop a targeted, relatively inexpensive public relations/communications plan, to implement it, and to demonstrate your success to the library director, board, city council, and other decision-makers. Develop a goal for this plan that achieves the type of things that decision-makers tend to like, such as increases in circulation, gate count, or attendance. Then, next time, develop a slightly more expensive plan and increase your funding incrementally, each time sharing your successes. Over time, chances are that the funders will see that the small investment in public relations activities is worth the increased use of the library, the changed public perception of the library's value, and the positive impact that it has in times of crisis.

SCHOOL LIBRARIES

SUCCESS STORY

Bob Hadley is the school library media specialist at Kennedy Middle School. Kennedy serves 800 students, grades 6–8, in an economically disadvantaged neighborhood. This past school year, his public relations/communications goal was to encourage parents to visit the school library with their children in the afternoons and evenings to help the students with their homework and research and to take advantage of the parent collection. It is the end of the school year and Bob has seen a lot of success.

In September, when he first started keeping the library open two evenings per week, eight parents visited per evening. As the school year progressed and Bob implemented his plan, attendance increased to 50 parents per open evening—and one night a record 102 parents visited the library with their children.

Bob is also exhausted. In January, he lost the funding for the library assistant who helped him during the evening hours. He had to recruit and train two volunteers to help. Throughout the school year, he continued to serve on the school-based management team and to meet with the teaching teams from each grade level on a regular basis. He also coached the school's basketball team.

In April, Bob's principal decided that there aren't sufficient funds to keep the library open in the evenings next school year. The parents who had taken advantage of the library's services spoke up and the teachers that Bob worked with went to the school-based management team and suggested other areas in the school's budget that could be cut. The result was that the principal made some budget adjustments and the Kennedy Middle School library will be open three nights per week next year and Bob will have a library assistant—in addition to his two volunteers—to help out on all of those evenings.

SCHOOL LIBRARY PR CHALLENGES

The school library media specialist faces the same challenge of finding time for public relations activities as public librarian, Susan Miller, in her success story. However, Susan is given some release time for her work and Bob Hadley has to take on whatever public relations work he wants to get done in addition to his duties as a member of the school's instructional team. Yet, similar to the public library's circumstances, ongoing public relations for a school library may be the key to its survival in times of budget cuts. The national guidelines for school library media programs, *Information Power*, includes this description of the overwhelming public relations responsibilities of school library media specialists: "Library media specialists must effectively publicize available services and resources, visibly serve on school and district-wide committees, actively participate in community projects, and clearly demonstrate the importance of the library media program in education."[1]

Library media specialists face the challenge of promoting the value of their programs in the community and also in their building and school districts. As the success story demonstrates, it is important to do such promotion on a consistent basis and not just when there are questions about whether or not to fund the school library media program.

Today, school districts are being seduced by technology. Some people think that the resources and role of the school library media program can be replaced by computers, Internet access, and a technology coordinator. Or the district administration may view the role of the school librarian as one of checking out and shelving books and may decide that volunteers or clerical staff can take care of those tasks, thus eliminating the need for the more expensive school library media specialist position. As a result, school library media specialists are often in the position of having to do "personal public relations." They must be vigilant about promoting the value of their role in the instructional program. They need to continue to learn about new technology and to become resources for both teachers and students in those areas.

The challenge is that school library media specialists often become so busy doing the work that they forget to spread the word. In addition to being contributing members of the school's instructional team, school library media specialists must be "self-promoters." They need to volunteer for school committees and to speak up when they have something to offer. They continually need to offer the library as a meeting place for the PTA, the school-based management team, or visitors from out of town. The energy of the school library media specialist must be focused on his or her work as an instructional leader in the school and not on checking out books and keeping them neatly shelved.

ACADEMIC LIBRARIES

SUCCESS STORY

When the Clarence University Library increased its open hours to 24 hours per day throughout the academic year, circulation librarian Kara Richardson was disappointed in the student response. The skeleton staff scheduled to work the 11 p.m.–7 a.m. shift was lucky if they saw five students during the evening, and the staff spent most of their time chatting and drinking coffee. Kara decided that the answer was to get the word out and she asked the library director if she could take on the responsibility of promoting the night-time hours in addition to her other duties. He readily agreed and Kara set about forming a public relations task force and developing and implementing a plan.

Only six weeks after the beginning of Kara's public relations activities, there were so many students in the library at 2 a.m. on a Wednesday morning that there weren't any seats left in the study rooms. Soon, the library director had to add staff to the night shift. By the next academic year, there were questions about whether or not the library could afford to continue its 24-hour schedule.

ACADEMIC LIBRARY PR CHALLENGES

Kara's public relations efforts were successful beyond what the fiscal resources of the university could support. This can also happen in other types of libraries. A service or program is promoted beyond what anyone can afford to provide. However, in this instance, when Kara began promoting the 24-hour schedule, the university's resources were being wasted as staff stood around whiling away the time. Chances are that if the night hours aren't available next academic year, the university will hear about it from its paying customers—the students. And the university understands that time and resources for studying are critical to the students' academic achievement which plays a role in the university's overall public relations efforts.

In some ways, academic libraries have more of a guaranteed place in their setting than school libraries do in theirs. In addition to providing resources for students, academic libraries often provide resources for faculty members who are engaging in "publish or perish" research projects. The struggle for the academic library is to maintain a balance between its role as a research center for students and faculty and a warm, welcoming place where students can study.

Like the other librarians described above, Kara added public relations activities to her other duties. The increases in circulation that may have occurred from the increased use at night, however, may have helped her as circulation librarian to lobby for more circulation staff.

Like school libraries, academic libraries also face the challenge of positioning themselves positively in their community as well as selling themselves to the students. Hosting special events, ensuring that there is a library presence at campus-wide events such as the homecoming parade, and attracting alumni donors are all activities that are time-consuming but important to a positive position. Academic libraries need to position themselves to prospective students as a drawing card; they should be a part of the admissions tour for prospective students and should be included in the university's recruitment material.

In addition, universities often offer their library as an enticing benefit in their "town and gown" relations programs, for example allowing members of the local community to use the library for no fee or for an extremely low fee. If this happens, the academic library immediately gains another audience, and it will need to design public relations activities to address that audience. Not only will the library face the challenge of promoting its services to this new target audience, but it will have to deal with integrating this new group with the audience it currently serves. Faculty members and students who are in the library studying and conducting research may not be too enthusiastic when people from the neighborhood visit just to look around. A public relations/ communications program that includes tours, orientation sessions, and other activities for this new audience will help the library meet this challenge.

SPECIAL LIBRARIES

SUCCESS STORY

Tom Patrick is the head librarian at the corporate library of the Princefield Environmental Engineering group. He leads a staff of two librarians and four clerical staff members who provide library service and research assistance for the group's 200 engineers. Tom's recent internal public relations challenge was to get the engineers to understand that they could request that materials be purchased for the library. (His predecessor considered himself an expert on environmental engineering and took it upon himself to make all of the collection development decisions.)

Six months ago, Tom approached his staff and suggested that they develop a public relations/communications plan to communicate their willingness to work with the firm's engineers to develop a collection that will best meet their needs. At first, the staff thought Tom was crazy. They told him that Princefield was a small firm and all he needed to do was send out a memo. But Tom asked them to give his idea a chance and to work with him on the plan's development. The group skeptically worked with Tom on the plan's development and initial implementation. After the first few weeks of enthusiastic response, they began to think about ideas for future internal public relations activities. Not only did the engineers begin to bring their purchase requests to Tom, but he eventually formed a selection committee of engineers from different areas of expertise in the firm.

Use of the Princefield Corporate Library and its resources has increased by 25 percent because now the materials more closely meet the engineers' needs. And the president of Princefield has increased the library's collection development budget by $150,000 because the heads of the firm's departments recommended that their small departmental reference materials budgets be pooled for the library to purchase materials for everyone's use.

SPECIAL LIBRARY PR CHALLENGES

Special libraries can disappear from the corporate landscape if they don't make themselves an integral part of the organization's operations. Like Tom's library, they can increase their funding and services if they prove that the service they provide is critical to the work of others in the organization. In some ways, they are in a position that public, academic, and school libraries might envy. Their budgets can be increased as the organization's revenues and their perceived value increases. On the other hand, they can also be cut or eliminated also and there isn't a large community to rally to their aid. If the special library hasn't proven its value in the past, a quick public relations campaign probably isn't going to help. Therefore, ongoing, consistent public relations activities are critical to the survival of special libraries, just as they are to public, school, and academic libraries.

SHARED PUBLIC RELATIONS CHALLENGES

Different types of libraries do indeed face some different challenges to their public relations/communications activities. But in many ways, they share a lot of the same obstacles. School, public, academic, and special libraries are all institutions that strive to provide the highest quality of service to their users. All four face the hard choices of which services to promote and to whom, which programs to fund and why; and they must all find that delicate balance between promoting and over-promising. In addition, all four types of libraries often exist within the context of a larger organization. School libraries are in schools in school districts; public libraries are often a department of a city or county government; academic libraries are part of a college or university; and special libraries are part of the organization that they serve. As a result their public relations/communications activities often come under the auspices of these larger organizations. The freedom to develop and implement their own plans may not exist under these circumstances. In fact, a library's public relations activities might be stymied by the larger organization so that its other public relations goals can be met. This is a difficult challenge to face. The only answer is to begin with a strong internal public relations program designed to demonstrate to the larger organization the positive perception that the library can help create for everyone, and then to build incrementally.

Developing and disseminating a clear, consistent message is another challenge for all types of libraries. No matter how hard the people developing and implementing the public relations plan might try, there are many obstacles along the way to disseminating the message to the target audience. A library board member might go to the press and tell a story that is the exact opposite of the one you are trying to spread. A parent challenging a book in the school library puts an entirely different spin on the community outreach program that the school library media specialist is trying to implement. The key here is patience and education. Bringing as many people on board in the development and implementation of your public relations plan as possible will help you to avoid such obstacles. They will still happen, but the people who understand and support your message will help you deflect the conflicting story.

Another challenge for all public relations professionals, especially those in libraries and nonprofit organizations, is time. As demonstrated in the success stories above, librarians are often asked to develop and implement public relations activities in addition to their other duties, with little or no release time. They get stressed out and begin to realize that, as public awareness and library use increases, all that their success brings is more work. This is a critical issue and can only be solved by working to persuade library directors and other decision-makers to make public relations a priority by devoting staff time to it. School library-media specialists must establish priorities for their workloads and put public relations at a higher level.

Finally, funding for public relations activities is a challenge faced in all types of libraries. Any library has limited funds and when the pot is divided public relations often gets short shrift. It is a difficult decision. If you don't fund collections and programs sufficiently, you won't have anything to promote. Yet, if the library's programs and collections aren't used by the community and viewed as important and valuable, the library's overall funding may be cut. Librarians must work hard to convince those who make the budget decisions that funding for public relations is essential to the organization's survival.

CONCLUSION

Libraries developing and implementing effective public relations plans may face a lot of challenges and obstacles. Yet, the rewards make the effort worth the battle. The goal of any library is to serve its community, and public relations activities are the key to creating public awareness of the availability and value of that service.

Effective public relations and communications take time and patience. There will be great leaps forward and steps backward, and there will be times when you will be ready to give up. But, no matter what type of library you are in, the investment of carefully developed, ongoing, and consistent public relations for your library will eventually pay off. Your constituency will increase its use of your library's programs and resources. Users will come to your defense during funding crises and intellectual freedom challenges. They will view your library as a "community value."

NOTE

1. American Library Association and Association for Educational Communications and Technology, *Information Power: Guidelines for School Library Media Programs* (Chicago: American Library Association, 1988), 53.

14 EVALUATING YOUR EFFORTS

You are finished! You have developed and implemented your communications plan within the time frame that you originally designated. You completed all of your activities in order to meet your objectives and you made the midcourse corrections that you deemed necessary. There is nothing left to do, right? Wrong! The next step is critical for planning future communications efforts. You need to look with a critical eye at what you accomplished and evaluate your efforts.

Your public relations/communications plan is the key to your evaluation. While it provided the road map for your efforts during implementation, it will also provide you with a mechanism for looking at what you did and determining what worked and what should be improved or changed in the future. Remember, however, that public relations is not an exact science. It is subjective, and your evaluation of your efforts will also be subjective. Without investing large amounts of money in survey research, it will be hard to determine whether or not you have actually changed public perception of your library and its services. Determining this will be easier in a more isolated environment, such as a school or university library, as opposed to a public library system that serves a large community. Careful study of your success in meeting your public relations/communications goals and objectives will provide you with useful information for future planning, no matter how large your target audience might be.

When evaluating your program, it is important to remember that the number of newsletters or flyers produced and the number of news releases mailed are not effective measures of success. You want to think of evaluating your efforts in terms of people, not things. The guiding question for your entire evaluation should be: "How have people behaved differently as a result of our efforts?"

You will also want to evaluate your efforts in terms of adherence to your plan. That doesn't mean that taking advantage of public relations opportunities, such as the passage of a library bond issue in a nearby community, aren't valid efforts, but you must consider how much such opportunities interrupted or affected progress toward your public relations goal.

EVALUATION ANXIETY

For some reason, many of us suffer from evaluation anxiety. We view any kind of evaluation as a judgment that says "you succeeded" or "you failed." However, as mentioned above, public relations is an inexact science and there really are no blatant successes or failures. There is always something you could improve upon and there is always something that was done exceptionally well. In addition, the accomplishment of any library's public relations/communications goal never rests on the shoulders of one individual or group; it is a team effort that involves all of the players who are part of the library's community. In a public library, the work towards the goal is accomplished through all of the staff, the director, the board, volunteers, the city administration, and the community-at-large. In a school, it is the entire faculty, the principal, the PTA, the students, parents, volunteers, and others who contribute to the success of the public relations program—not just the school library media specialist working in isolation.

Evaluation is an opportunity to look critically at what we accomplished so that we can all do things even better in the future.

TIMING YOUR EVALUATION

Evaluating your communications efforts after you have completed them seems logical. However, depending on your goal and the time frame that you designated to complete it, you may wish to conduct some "formative" evaluation efforts at various times during implementation of your plan. For example, if your efforts are directed at obtaining additional funding for your library and the decision will be made on a specific date by a designated group of people (for example, a bond issue election or a school board budget meeting), assessing your efforts during implementation will help you make midcourse corrections, before it's too late. In other situations, your goal may be broader and more intangible, such as "Create the public perception that Middletown Public Library is a community center." You know that the time frame for achieving this goal is relatively long and that there isn't a specific end date; evaluating your public relations/communications activities at the end of the designated time frame or on an annual basis is more practical.

Even if you plan to evaluate your efforts at the completion of your plan, you will want to start planning and conducting the evaluation before the end of your time frame. You don't want to reach a time when your communications activities stop just because the time frame for your plan ended. Implementing two plans in succession at a time would help avoid this situation, but you want to be sure that the plans overlap so that the community and press continue to hear from you while you are evaluating your efforts.

You can use the same techniques for evaluating your public relations/communications efforts no matter when you assess your accomplishments. Evaluation techniques include revisiting your public relations/communications plan and implementing the evaluation technique that you included in your plan, working with other library and school staff to discuss perceptions, and perhaps engaging in some of the research activities that you used in your planning process.

REVISITING YOUR PUBLIC RELATIONS/ COMMUNICATIONS PLAN

Pull out that public relations/communications plan. It should look pretty well used, like any road map after a long journey. Tattered a bit, torn, and covered with your notes and marks, it will guide you through the evaluation process just as it guided you through your communications activities.

The final element in your plan should describe a process for evaluating your efforts. Look carefully at that item. Now after implementing your efforts, is that still the most effective way to assess your accomplishments? Will it really tell you what happened, or do you need to think about other factors? Chances are that the technique you described will play a major role in your overall evaluation of your efforts, but you may wish to gain information for future efforts.

If you worked with a library-wide task force or committee to plan and implement your public relations/communications plan, you should involve that group in the evaluation process. The discussion in this group about what you achieved and what still needs work may be some of the most valuable information you will gain. Bring them together and talk about plans for evaluation. Ask them what they would suggest. Should they be the group that leads the evaluation of the efforts they planned or do they recommend that you form a different staff committee?

Remember, however, that even before you evaluate, your planning committee needs to celebrate! You worked hard implementing your public relations/communications plan and you should celebrate your accomplishments.

Whether you decide to evaluate your efforts by committee or, for reasons of practicality, by yourself, your evaluation should answer several key questions.

- **What did you set out to accomplish?**
  The answer to this question is simple. It is your public relations goal, your message, and your target audience. Reaching a specific audience with a particular message to achieve your goal is what you set out to accomplish.

- **What did you do to accomplish it?**
  To answer this question, carefully review your public relations/communications plan. Look at each activity and each objective. Did you complete each activity? Why or why not? Do you have samples of your work (for example, newsletters, photos from a special event, newspaper clippings)? Whether or not you completed all of the activities under an objective, did you achieve the objective? In your opinion, why or why not? Think about whether or not you were too ambitious when planning your activities.

- **Did you choose the right message? Did you communicate the message you chose?**
  Look carefully at the message that you wanted to communicate. Did it really say what you wanted? Did you really communicate it through your public relations activities? Is it still a relevant message that should be part of your future communications efforts?

- **Was your target audience the appropriate one for your message and your activities?**
  The target audience might have been the right one for the message you wanted to communicate, but your activities might not have matched your audience. For example, if your target audience was senior citizens and you wanted them to know that they can use the library's services without leaving their homes, it might seem logical that electronic communications would be a good tool for reaching them.

But you wouldn't achieve your goal if only 5 percent of the senior citizens in your community have a computer or access to a computer. Think about whether or not your audience, your message, and your activities worked together.

- **Did you accomplish your goal? Or how much progress did you make toward achieving your goal?**
  This question will be either very easy or extremely difficult to answer. For example, consider a finite goal, such as one in the sample school library public relations/communications plan on page 197: "Communicate to parents, teachers, and school board members the role that the Internet can play in education for children. Demonstrate the Internet's valuable educational resources in order to secure funding for Internet services in the school library media center by June 1997." By June 1997, you will have a "yes" or "no" answer to the question "Did we accomplish our goal?" However, if your goal is the broader—"Create the public perception that Middletown Public Library is a community center"—the question may be more difficult to answer and your answer may be more subjective. Research, such as you may have conducted in your planning process, may be necessary to answer the question in this instance.

- **What happened during the implementation of your plan that you didn't anticipate?**
  This question is a particularly good one for your planning committee to consider. The group should think about "What kinds of serendipitous events contributed to our movement toward our public relations goal?" and "What kinds of events interrupted progress toward our goal?" For example, a snowy winter may have interrupted the school's progress toward secure funding for Internet services because all of the special events that the librarian had planned to demonstrate the technology were canceled because of weather. Or maybe the new station manager at the local television station who arrived during the implementation of your plan loves libraries and insisted that his 6 p.m. newscast carry at least one library story per week. Both of these events are out of the library's control, but they may have had an impact on progress towards the library's public relations goals.

- **How are things different now compared to before you implemented your public relations/communications plan?**
  The answer to this question may or may not have a relationship to your efforts. If your school has a new principal or your city has a new mayor, that is a change in the environment in which your efforts were implemented. If your library's gate count has increased by 125 percent, some of that increase may be attributed to your efforts; but some increase might also be attributed to the fact that two of your branch libraries were closed for three months for renovation. Think about changes in personnel, changes in environment, changes in behavior, and changes in perceptions that have occurred during the implementation of your plan. Then, decide which of the changes can be attributed, in some part, to your efforts.

- **What will you do differently in the future? What will you do the same way?**
  Think carefully about what worked and what didn't. Maybe you developed a wonderful Web page to promote your library's services, but you didn't put the URL on your promotional materials. Or maybe you sent out so many news releases that the press felt inundated and didn't cover your library at all. Think about what you did right and what you would change. The answers to this question will provide important information for planning your future efforts.

Prepare a document based on the group's discussion or your consideration of these questions. This is a qualitative evaluation of your public relations/communications efforts. You may also wish to ask three or four other library staff or members of your Friends of the Library group to answer the same questions. While the answers may seem highly subjective to you, they will provide valuable information for planning your future public relations/communications efforts—and they may provide ammunition for when you have to ask the library board or other administrative body for funding for future efforts.

EVALUATION RESEARCH

If you used research during your planning process, you may wish to replicate that research when evaluating your work. This will provide you with quantitative information to use to assess your efforts and plan for the future.

Holding focus groups of the same size and demographic breakdown as those used during your planning process and guiding the participants through the same questioning process will provide you with some insight into whether or not public perception of your library has changed. Conducting the same survey—in the same location—that you used to assess perceptions during the planning process will also provide you with a perspective on changed perceptions.

WHAT NEXT?

The next step is to go back to Chapter 2 and start all over again by developing and implementing your next public relations/communications efforts. Your next plan may simply be an extension of the plan that you just completed, with an extended time frame and some changes in the activities based on your experiences; or, if you had a finite goal and achieved it, you may develop a plan with an entirely different focus.

The important thing to remember is that no matter how close or far you were in achieving your goal, your experiences during the implementation of your previous plan should inform your future efforts. Changing public perceptions and communicating your library's message to your target audiences is a building process. It is not a one-shot deal! You can't say "Been there, done that." It is a cyclical process of assessment, planning, implementation, and evaluation. Each time you go through the process, you will learn a little more, understand your audience a little better, and improve on your efforts.

APPENDIX A: PUBLIC RELATIONS/ COMMUNICATIONS PLAN

OUTLINE

Goal: What is the purpose of this plan? What do you want to achieve?

Time Frame: What is the implementation period for this plan? It might be six months or two years, depending on what you want to achieve. The broader your goal, the more time and energy will be required to achieve it.

Major Target Audience: Who do you primarily want to communicate with? Promote your services to?

Minor Target Audiences: Who is the secondary audience for this plan? Do you want your library colleagues in other communities to know what you are doing?

Objectives and Activities

A. Objective
You can have as many objectives as you want. The number depends on how broad your goal is and what it will take to achieve it. Promoting use of the video collection to children may take only three simple objectives with a few supporting activities. Communicating the services and programs of your entire system to the community might involve 20 objectives with 10 activities each. The key is to keep the plan manageable. Don't set yourself up to not complete it. Examine each objective and its supporting activities and think carefully about the human and fiscal resources needed to complete each one.

Time Frame: It is important to describe the time frame for the completion of each objective. Some objectives might continue for the full time frame of your public relations/communications plan. Others will be completed at various times during the implementation of the plan.

Person Responsible: For each objective in your plan it should be specified who has overall responsibility for seeing that this objective is achieved. The person responsible may not accomplish the objective alone, but he or she is the accountable individual. This is particularly important if you are in a library without a designated public relations or communications staff person.

1. **Activities:** Activities are what you will do to achieve the objective. Think carefully about what communications tools or strategies might best help you achieve the objective. Such activities as newsletters, flyers, and news releases support communications objectives, and so do displays and public speaking engagements. Now is a good time, as you are developing your activities, to review carefully the results of your research. What did people say about the things you are already doing? Did the majority of the people that you interviewed say that your newsletter was too cute and didn't include enough information about services? If so, your activity might be to change the focus of your newsletter, rather than to create a whole new newsletter.

    Time Frame: Each activity should be assigned a time frame within the time period designated for completion of the objective.

    Person Responsible: You may wish to designate the person responsible for each activity—unless it is the person responsible for the overall objective.

    Evaluation: Describe how you will evaluate your plan's success. For example, rather than simply reviewing the plan to make sure you completed each activity, it might be more effective to conduct another survey or hold another round of focus groups to see if you really succeeded in changing perceptions.

SAMPLES

SAMPLE: SCHOOL LIBRARY

Goal: Communicate to parents and school board members the role that the Internet can play in education for children. Demonstrate the Internet's valuable educational resources in order to secure funding for Internet services in the school library media center by June 1997.

Time Frame: September 1996–June 1997

Major Target Audiences: Parents of students enrolled in our school

Teachers

School board members

Minor Target Audiences: Other community members

Objectives and Activities

A. **Objective:** Plan, promote, and host two brown-bag teacher lunches per month in the school library media center. Use the time to demonstrate Internet resources in particular curriculum areas. Cover a different subject (such as space, rain forests, music, or art) each time.

Time Frame: September–December 1996

Person Responsible: School library media specialist

   1. **Activity:** Publish item announcing lunches in bimonthly faculty newsletter.

   Time Frame: September and November 1996

   Person Responsible: School library media specialist

   2. **Activity:** Produce and distribute to all faculty members a flyer announcing each lunch and the topic that will be the focus of the Internet demonstration.

Time Frame: September and November 1996

Person Responsible: School library media specialist

3. **Activity:** Develop and distribute a questionnaire evaluating the luncheon series and use the responses to develop a spring series.

    Time Frame: December 1996

    Person Responsible: School library media specialist

B. **Objective:** Work with students to develop and present a demonstration of Internet resources at Parent's Night in January.

    Time Frame: September 1996–January 1997

    Person Responsible: School library media specialist

    1. **Activity:** Identify teachers willing to have their students work on a research project using Internet resources. Work with them to plan and implement the project.

        Time Frame: September 1996–January 1997

        Person Responsible: School library media specialist and identified teachers

    2. **Activity:** Promote the demonstration in the library media center as a special feature of Parents Night by publishing an article in the school newsletter. Include information on the Parents Night flyer that is sent home with all students.

        Time Frame: January 1997

        Person Responsible: School library media specialist

    3. **Activity:** Encourage press coverage of the demonstration by sending a news release announcement to the local newspaper, and to the television and radio stations. Identify specific students for interviews with reporters.

        Time Frame: January 1997

        Person Responsible: School library media specialist and identified teachers

C. **Objective:** Work with teachers and principal to prepare and make a presentation to the school board demonstrating the availability of curriculum resources on the Internet and comparing the cost of computers and Internet connections to the cost of purchasing those resources on an annual basis. Use examples of student work and a live demonstration in the presentation.

Time Frame: September 1996–February 1997. Presentation is scheduled for March school board meeting.

Person Responsible: School library media specialist and identified teachers and students

1. **Activity:** Prepare a press kit that includes examples of student research using Internet resources and the cost comparison. Distribute to local media, announcing the presentation at the school board meeting.

    Time Frame: February 1997

    Person Responsible: School library media specialist working with district communications director

2. **Activity:** Provide a copy of the press kit to each school board member and all PTA board members.

    Time Frame: February 1997

    Person Responsible: School library media specialist

3. **Activity:** Schedule a minimum of five other times to repeat this presentation, including to a PTA meeting and meetings of such community groups as the Rotary or Kiwanis.

    Time Frame: March–June 1997

    Person Responsible: School library media specialist and identified teachers and students

    Evaluation: Prior to implementing this plan, we will survey the teachers, parents, and school board members about their perceptions of the value of Internet resources in the curriculum. Following the completion of the plan, we will repeat the survey and compare results. In addition, the true measurement of the plan's success will be if, at the June 1997 budget meeting, the school board approves our request for funds to purchase additional computers, install more phone lines, and increase Internet access.

SAMPLE: ACADEMIC LIBRARY

Goal:	Create faculty and student awareness of the university library's expanded hours by launching a multidimensional public relations campaign. Achieve a 15 percent increase in the library's overall gate count.
Time Frame:	September–December 1997
Major Target Audiences:	Faculty members and students
Minor Target Audiences:	University staff

Objectives and Activities

A. **Objective:** Inform all students and faculty of the new library night hours by developing and implementing a "Night Owl" study-hour campaign.
    Time Frame: August–December 1997
    Person Responsible: Manager of reference services

    1. **Activity:** Develop a logo and slogan for the "Night Owl" campaign.

    Time Frame: August 1997

    Person Responsible: Manager of reference services working with university graphic designer

    2. **Activity:** Design and print a magnet using the campaign logo and art and listing the library's new hours and phone numbers. Distribute to all students and faculty via the campus mail.

    Time Frame: August 1997

    Person Responsible: Manager of reference services

    3. **Activity:** Develop posters using "Night Owl" artwork and listing library hours. Post in all dorms and university buildings.

Time Frame: August–September 1997

Person Responsible: Manager of reference services

4. **Activity:** Write and send a press release to the campus paper and television and radio stations announcing the new library hours.

   Time Frame: August 1997

   Person Responsible: Manager of reference services

5. **Activity:** Plan, promote, and host a midnight open house at the library during mid-term exams. Promote via flyers in all student and faculty mailboxes, on campus bulletin boards, and as an insert in the campus newspaper. Provide students with refreshments and additional magnets listing the library's hours and phone numbers.

   Time Frame: October 1997

   Person Responsible: Manager of reference services

B. **Objective:** Work with the campus newspaper to develop a regular weekly feature on "Night Owls at the Library," focusing on the unique adventures of students who take advantage of our night hours. Highlight the advantages of studying at night.

Time Frame: September–December 1997

Person Responsible: Manager of reference services

1. **Activity:** Identify a student reporter interested in the library and its services. Provide the reporter with a special tour and orientation.

   Time Frame: September 1997

   Person Responsible: Manager of reference services

2. **Activity:** Work with the reporter to identify students to be featured in the "Night Owls" column.

   Time Frame: September–December 1997

   Person Responsible: Manager of reference services

C. **Objective:** Promote the library, its new hours, and its resources to university faculty.

Time Frame: August–September 1997

Person Responsible: Manager of reference services

1. **Activity:** Develop a packet of information about the library and its services and resources for all university faculty members. Include a suggestion slip and a request form to add materials to the collection.

   Time Frame: August 1997

   Person Responsible: Manager of reference services

2. **Activity:** Have the packet for each faculty member hand-delivered by the librarian responsible for library service in that faculty member's subject area.

   Time Frame: August–September 1997

   Person Responsible: Manager of reference services working with librarians

   Evaluation: Prior to the implementation of this plan, a brief survey of 100 students and 50 faculty, assessing their perceptions of library services and resources, was conducted. Following the fall semester, this survey will be repeated. In addition, gate counts for the previous fall semester will be compared to this fall to determine if the promotion resulted in increased use. The targeted increase is 15 percent.

BIBLIOGRAPHY

American Library Association and Association for Educational Communications and Technology. *Information Power: Guidelines for School Library Media Programs.* Chicago: ALA Books, 1988.

Associated Press Stylebook and Libel Manual. Reading, Mass.: Addison-Wesley Publishing Company, 1995.

Beach, Mark. *Newsletter Sourcebook.* Cincinnati, Ohio: North Light Books, 1993.

Blake, Barbara Radke, and Barbara L. Stein. *Creating Newsletters, Brochures and Pamphlets: A How-to-Do-It Manual for School and Public Librarians.* New York: Neal-Schuman Publishers, 1992.

Drucker, Peter F. *Managing the Nonprofit Organization: Principles and Practices.* New York: Harper Collins, 1990.

Harris, Thomas L. *The Marketer's Guide to Public Relations: How Today's Top Companies Are Using the New PR to Gain a Competitive Edge.* New York: John Wiley & Sons, 1991.

Jones, Susan K. *Creative Strategy in Direct Marketing.* Lincolnwood, Ill.: NTC Business Books, 1991.

Karp, Rashelle S., ed. *Part-Time Public Relations with Full-Time Results: A PR Primer for Libraries.* Chicago: American Library Association, 1995.

Karpisek, Marian. *Policymaking for School Library Media Programs.* Chicago: American Library Association, 1989.

Lawrence Ragan Communications. "Use Electronic Bulletin Boards to Improve Every Aspect of Your Communication Function," *Technology for Communicators: Ideas for Communicating in a Wired World.* Chicago: Lawrence Ragen Communications, n.d.): 2.

Levison, Jay Conrad, and Charles Rubin. *Guerrilla Marketing Online: The Entrepeneur's Guide to Earning Profits on the Internet.* New York: Houghton Mifflin, 1995.

McCune, Bonnie F., and Charleszine Nelson. *Managing Volunteers in Libraries: A How-to-Do-It Manual.* New York: Neal-Schuman Publishers, 1995.

Metz, Ray E. and Gail Junion-Metz. *Using the World Wide Web and Creating Home Pages: A How-to-Do-It Manual for Librarians.* New York: Neal-Schuman Publishers, 1996.

Nash, Edward L., ed. *The Direct Marketing Handbook.* New York: McGraw-Hill, 1992.

Negroponte, Nicholas. *Being Digital.* New York: Random House, 1995.

Peters, Tom. *The Pursuit of WOW! Every Person's Guide to Topsy-Turvy Times.* New York: Random House, 1994.

Public Interest Public Relations. *Promoting Issues and Ideas: A Guide to Public Relations for Nonprofit Organizations.* New York: The Foundation Center, 1987.

Roberts, Anne F., and Susan Griswold Blandy. *Public Relations for Librarians.* Englewood, CO.: Libraries Unlimited, 1989.

Saffir, Leonard. *Power Public Relations: How to Get PR to Work for You.* Lincolnwood, Ill.: NTC Business Books, 1994.

Wagner, Mary M., and Suzanne H. Mahmoodi. *A Focus Group Interview Manual.* Chicago: American Library Association, 1994.

Walters, Suzanne. *Marketing: A How-to-Do-It Manual for Librarians.* New York: Neal-Schuman Publishers, 1992.

Yale, David R. *The Publicity Handbook: How to Maximize Publicity for Products, Services and Organizations.* Lincolnwood, Ill.: NTC Business Books, 1992.

INDEX

COLOPHON

Lisa A. Wolfe is a Vice President at Marcy Monyek and Associates, Inc., a Chicago-based public relations agency. She has 12 years of public relations and communications experience in public and school libraries.

After working briefly as a newspaper reporter in northern Idaho, Wolfe began her career in libraries in 1985 as the Public Information Officer for Spokane Public Library, Spokane, Washington. She developed the position into the senior level administrative post of Manager of Community Relations. Highlights of her accomplishments during her eight year tenure included developing and implementing a major capital campaign and earning numerous awards for public relations, promotions and communications, including two of the American Library Association's prestigious John Cotton Dana Awards for Outstanding Library Public Relations.

Wolfe also created the position of Coordinator of Communications for the American Association of School Librarians (AASL), a division of the American Lirabry Association(ALA). In addition to managing the communications efforts of this division, she developed and implemented communications strategies for the National Library Power Program, a $45 million dollar school library improvement initiative, funded by the DeWitt Wallace-Reader's Digest Fund and managed by AASL. She was the lead staff person working on AASL's two membership intiatives, ICONnect and Count on Reading.

Prior to her position at Marcy Monyek and Associates, Wolfe was the Manager of the Chicago Public Schools Department of Libraries and Information Services, where she coordinated the set-up and opening of the school system's new professional library and assisted in the development of the department. Wolfe has been active in ALA and the Washington Library Association. She served as the editor of *ALKI: The Journal of the Washington Library Association* for three years.

She has a bachelor of arts in journalism and a master of arts in organizational leadership from Gonzaga University in Spokane.